Women in Leadership

Living Beyond Challenges

11 Stories of Courage and Triumph

Compiled by

Dr. Amanda H. Goodson
& Dr. Yvette Rice

Women in Leadership – Living Beyond Challenges
Compiled by Dr. Amanda H. Goodson and Dr. Yvette Rice
Featured authors (in alphabetical order)
Dr. Amanda Goodson
Dr. Yvette Rice
Rosalind Longmire
Dr. Jana Lovelace
Jeannie Lynch
Jana Monroe
Melissa Morrison-Ellis
Catherine Ripley
Odetta Scott
Sharon Wamble-King
Amarie Whetten

© 2019 by Amanda H. Goodson and Yvette Rice
All rights reserved.

Editing: Adam Colwell's WriteWorks, LLC, Adam Colwell and Ginger Colwell
Book Design: Inktobook.com
Published by Amanda Goodson Global, LLC

Printed in the United States of America
ISBN (Paperback): 978-1-951501-00-6
ISBN (eBook): 978-1-951501-01-3

Acknowledgments

....

WE ARE GRATEFUL for how Jesus brought together such a wonderful group of women to share their incredible stories.

Dr. Amanda Goodson

To my husband, Lonnie, for his full dedication and support; my son, Jelonni, for his encouragement and faithfulness; my mom for her kind words; and my sister for being there through thick and thin. I would additionally like to acknowledge all of the ladies who fearlessly challenged themselves to get this work done. They did it with a great attitude and much love for the Lord. Also, I am excited to acknowledge Je're Harmon who is so dedicated to the work of the ministry to which she is called. She has a "yes" in her spirit and an attitude of a Kingdom saint. I am encouraged and grateful!

Dr. Yvette Rice

To God, who gets all of the glory and honor. Without Him, I could do nothing. A loving thank you, too, to Dr. Amanda Goodson for pursuing the vision of this wonderful anthology.

Thank you to all of the women who so boldly shared their stories of challenges and triumphs that made this book possible.

A special thank you to my husband, Bishop Sam Rice, for encouraging me to spread my wings and soar to my God-given destiny. Also, to our children, Sharné, Samuel Christopher, and Amber: thank you for your loving support.

Rosalind Longmire

To God; my husband, Al Longmire; my children, Pierce and Jarrett; my mother, Charsie Hunter; my sisters, Delma Hawkins and Marva Cooksey; and, finally, Dr. Amanda Goodson, my friend, coach, and mentor.

Dr. Jana Lovelace

To my love, John Lovelace. Life with you is an adventure and I am so glad God saw fit to let me borrow you for a lifetime. I love being your wife above all things. Because of you, we are "living the dream." To my three "little loves," John William, Locke, and Liza Kate—you make our lives full! I am so thankful that you are mine and I am yours, forever and always. I could not love you more! To my mom, my first fan and biggest cheerleader! And to my partner in crime, Jeannie Lynch, there is no one else I would join on this excursion! Buckle up, sister! It's going to be a fun ride.

Jeannie Lynch

To God, who I give all the glory! I am so thankful for the like-minded women He has put in my life! Kathy Melton, Starla Such, Dr. Jana Lovelace, Kelly Dutton, Dr. Yvette Rice, Kitty Joe, Jessica Clark, and Jan Murphy. Finally, to the entire Sprout

Tribe who have allowed me to lead them and truly learn what it means to be a leader. I love you all!

Jana Monroe

To my husband, Dale Monroe, for believing in my abilities to the extent that I also began believing in them!

Melissa Morrison-Ellis

To my husband for his love, guidance, and patience accompanying me through this season. Continued blessings.

Catherine Ripley

To my two children, Candace Ripley and Alex Ripley. They are my heart, my soul, my compass, my beacons, and my purpose. To my mother, Candace Hiroko McGurk, who taught me kindness, and to my father, William J. McGurk, who taught me how to never take "no" for an answer. I am also forever grateful to my two high school music teachers who taught me that magic, music, and emotion should all happen together, often, and loudly. To all of my military leaders, fellow officers, and sailors—it truly wasn't just a job, but an unbelievable adventure. Thank you for every minute! Finally, many thanks to Dr. Amanda Goodson, whose leadership, mentorship, and friendship make the world a better place.

Odetta Scott

To my husband, parents, family, and friends. Having you in my corner to provide support has proved invaluable. Thank you all so very much!

Sharon Wamble-King

To my husband, Leon, for his unwavering love, support, fervent prayers, and effusively championing his vision of my unlimited possibilities. To my family, those of blood and love, whose prayers, loyal allegiance, acceptance and, of course, humor are continual sources of encouragement, inspiration, comfort, and joy. To my sister-friends—you know who you are—who stand by and with me, cheering me and challenging me as I navigate through every chapter of my journey. I am so grateful for your love, gracious generosity, vulnerability, insightful conversations, walking, sitting, and divinely pausing with me along my winding life path. To my mentors, coaches, and professional colleagues whose belief in my brilliance creates the safety and provides the catalyst for me to challenge my thinking, learn, grow, and evolve. To my Ph.D. colleagues who catapult me to new intellectual vistas. Most importantly, I am grateful to God, who has a plan for my life, one for good and not disaster, to give me a future and a hope. He has begun a good work in me, and He will complete it.

Amarie Whetten

To my husband, our family's MVP. He remains my calm, warm place to nestle into during life's adventures. I always wanted to have a big family and am grateful to have these: Kate, Leah, Sophie, and Kyle. I appreciate Kate's curiosity, support, and openness to new adventures. Leah has a giving heart, warm smile, and is one of the most perceptive people I know. Sophie is non-stop entertainment and constantly coming up with inspiring words of wisdom. Kyle reminds us that the most important thing to do today is go running around outside and snuggle with the people you love. To my parents, Julia and Claude, who have supported our ventures every step of the way and even moved close to us to help with the kids so we had some bandwidth to work on our dreams. To my brother, Steve, and his wife, Kelda, and sister, Annelise, and her husband, Jesse, who continue to play such a huge role in my life. I loved sharing a childhood with them and love even more how our current relationships continue to sustain us. I'm also grateful to the Groth family (Megan, Cory, Payton, and Addison) for the decades of a friendship like no other. We keep moving across the country to be together. Thank you to the "Girl Band" for the weekly connection and pep talks; Nicole Quackenbush for always cheering me on and being the number-one problem solver; and to my longtime friend, Carl Cicero, for modeling a happy life. I'm grateful to the Whetten family, especially my mother-in-law, Janet, for being a strong role model and teacher. We miss my father-in-law, Dorel, for his warmth and talent for bringing peace to any situation. To the growing Juice Plus+ Wellness Warrior team, who give me light, inspiration, and connection. They are the most amazing tribe a person could ask for. I would not be here had it not been for the many mentors, coaches, and friends who have impacted my life. Finally, I am grateful for my faith and am awaiting the next tap on the shoulder from God.

Table of Contents

Take Your Place

....

THERE'S NO DOUBT the words of Jesus Christ are important—but they are especially significant when they're directed at you.

In His Sermon on the Mount, the Lord said this to each and every one of you:

> "You're here to be light, bringing out the God-colors in the world. God is not a secret to be kept. We're going public with this, as public as a city on a hill. If I make you light-bearers, you don't think I'm going to hide you under a bucket, do you? I'm putting you on a light stand. Now that I've put you there on a hilltop, on a light stand—shine! Keep open house; be generous with your lives. By opening up to others, you'll prompt people to open up with God, this generous Father in heaven." (Matthew 5:14-16, The Message)

Throughout Scripture, God strategically placed women in specific places and times to bring about remarkable change for His people and the world. Some were mentioned by name—Rebekah, Rahab, Deborah, Ruth, Esther, Hannah—while others were unnamed but are forever remembered for their actions: the Shunammite woman, the Canaanite woman, or the Samaritan woman at the well, to mention a few.

Although God placed the spotlight on the lives of these diverse women, their assignments did not come without challenges. Yet each one had divine purpose and contributed in writing the history of Christ Himself.

In this hour, we believe the Lord has a specific assignment for each one of you to be light bearers who change the lives of people in your circles of influence. You are here, right now, to shine for His glory!

Women in Leadership – Living Beyond Challenges will introduce you to 11 remarkable women whose unique stories of courage, tenacity, and triumph will elevate and inspire you to take your place with them in bringing about remarkable change for Him in your world.

Jeannie Lynch once lived in a way that was heading to certain destruction after enduring abuse, rejection, rape, and a family suicide. Then a jail cell encounter with the living God started turning her life around so that today she has healed the wounds of her past and has freedom to lead others to their own breakthroughs. Her life lessons will show you how to lead and be free.

Catherine Ripley has found herself leading and being led by countless extraordinary people during a military and professional career highlighted by being the first woman from Montana and a member of the third class of women ever appointed to the U.S. Naval Academy. Her insights will allow you as a leader to find your rhythm and keep the beat going.

Rosalind Longmire tells her story of progressing from pioneering entrepreneur to pastor of her childhood church and watching how God put together the pieces of the puzzle of her life in the process. Her legacy of faith and lessons of perseverance will inspire you to see how you can become of a masterpiece of love created in God's image.

Dr. Amanda Goodson uses her incredible story of how she became the first African American woman ever to hold the position of Director of Safety and Mission Assurance at NASA, and faced one of her biggest personal trials, to now take on amazing and unexpected new leadership roles. She'll show you how your full potential as a leader is just waiting to emerge.

Jana Monroe discovered how her two life callings were fulfilled by an amazing 20-plus year career in the Federal Bureau of Investigation (FBI), culminating with her current position in global security. Her many firsts along the way gave her knowledge about leadership that she'll teach you so that you can recognize and take advantage of the situations that come your way.

Sharon Wamble-King unveils her journey of faith in the impossible as she talks about the predestination to excellence miraculously placed upon her as a child. You'll discover how she allowed it to be the foundation and inspiration for everything she's achieved and all that she teaches others about being a woman in leadership who can achieve the impossible.

Amarie Whetten reveals how her encounters with tragedy have helped her find her own personal wellness and happiness so that she can fulfill her passion to inspire others to achieve health and joy in their lives. You'll learn how to take pauses, reinvent yourself, and be fearless so you can overcome any challenge or obstacle that comes your way as a leader.

Melissa Morrison-Ellis tells how she developed a mindset of joy through a professional and spiritual journey that has seen her make a remarkable impact on others as she learned how to survive in the real world where acceptance is not freely given. She will inspire you to choose joy, sing your song, stay in the battle, and move beyond any obstacles that stand in your way.

Dr. Yvette Rice shares how she broke down a trio of walls to press through to her destiny to be a light for God in the marketplace and in the Christian church, all while helping others to learn to live in victory and excellence. She'll teach you how to take risks and knock down the walls that stand in the way of your pursuit of purpose.

Odetta Scott is driven to reach others by being an example and inspiring others to maximize their potential. Her story will reveal why she believes everything happens for a reason and show you why it's not as much about the direct value you bring, but about the greater impact you can have as a leader by developing others.

Dr. Jana Lovelace reveals how she used to follow one leader—herself—and how choosing to follow God instead led her from a life of learned busyness to one of fulfillment and freedom. Her literally death-defying tales will give you insights how you can love what you do while leading and loving others in pursuit of the passions God gave you.

Why is it vital for the Church, the people who make up the Body of Christ, and the world in general to have strong women in leadership? Women carry the seed and give birth to things in both the natural and spiritual realms. We saw this in the Bible with the stories of Elizabeth and Mary (Luke 1-2) in how they birthed John the Baptist and Jesus Christ in the natural while relying upon and supporting each other spiritually, carrying and sharing the seed of faith in God with one another. Elizabeth exclaimed, "As soon as the sound of your greeting reached my ears, the baby in my womb leaped for joy. Blessed is she who has believed that the Lord would fulfill his promises to her!" (Luke 1:44-45) We are called to do amazing things together that only we as women can achieve. We are becoming more influential in the Church and the world each day. Everywhere, women are being raised up by God for greatness! He also created us with a mantle of beauty spiritually and physically to emulate what the Church, the bride of Christ, is to Him and to His creation. It was no accident that the first people to see Jesus after He rose from the dead were women. They were the ones who shared the glorious news that He had risen!

This does not in any way detract from the role of men in the Church, the world, or our lives. God said, "It is not good for the man to be alone." (Genesis 2:18) He made women to partner with men, have relationship with men, and to go alongside men to create everything that God has made for His Kingdom. It is good for women to come and take their place of impact in what the Lord is doing in this season and in the history of eternity!

We also applaud our men who recognize, respect, and share the benefits of the role women have as leaders—and believe this book will wow you and inspire you to continue and grow in that role. Consider Barak who, when preparing to lead Israel in battle, said to Deborah, "If you go with me, I will go; but if you don't go with me, I won't go." (Judges 4:8) He knew he needed Deborah with him to achieve victory. Likewise, look at the favor and trust King Xerxes had for Esther when she boldly approached him to save her people from extinction. He saw her servant leadership and acted on her behalf.

Like Deborah and Esther, God has established and commissioned you to be a leader. Perhaps you don't quite recognize that yet—but by the time you finish *Women in Leadership - Living Beyond Challenges*, we believe the Lord will light a spark that will ignite into a flame where you'll say, "Yes, this is me. This is who I am!" Young women will be ready to step in the place God has for them, while older, seasoned women will be renewed with fresh oil for themselves and inspired to mentor, protect, and cover the younger women in their lives, just as Naomi did with Ruth. This is not the time to fade into the sunset. You are to be vibrant, active, and unlimited in what you still offer yourself and in how you can champion others.

Dear woman of God, you are awesome, wonderful and fearfully made (Psalm 139:14). You are an original who is vitally important to Him. The challenges to your destiny may be frustrating and even painful, but we believe they are building blocks and stepping stones into opportunities to bring transformation to others around you. The wilderness prunes you, shapes you, and sets you up for promotion and promise. What you share through your experience will become a legacy of victory and leadership passed on to others to help them discover and live out their purpose in Christ.

Get ready now to proclaim, without reservation or fear, "Lord, here I am! I want to be your light bearer. Where do you want me to shine?"

Read on—discover the answer, and take your place now.

Dr. Amanda H. Goodson
Dr. Yvette Rice

Other anthology books on topics such as the purpose and power of mentorship are available through Amanda Goodson Global, LLC.

1

Freedom to Lead

Jeannie Lynch

IT REALLY DOESN'T sound like much, stealing Coke bottles from behind an IGA store in Louisburg, North Carolina. But I was in college, I was drunk (yet again) and high, and the bottles were actually worth quite a bit of money back in 1978.

It was just the latest shenanigan that got me in trouble and sent me to jail—crazy, nonsensical behavior driven by addiction and depression—and there would be many more over the next 12 years before a DUI arrest, my third, landed me behind bars, knowing that I was looking at real prison time.

As the cell door clanged shut, I thought my life was over.

I didn't want it to be. Sure, I loathed myself. No, it was worse than that. I hated who I had become. But after everything I had been through—abuse, rejection, rape, a family suicide—it was no wonder I felt like I was the scum of the earth. Yet even then, I also knew there was someone deep down within me who truly cared about people. Even loved them. That conflict had waged within me ever since I could remember.

I plopped down onto the bunk in the cell, all by myself with no one to call, and no one at whom to point a finger. Addicts love to pass blame, but there was no one else to blame.

I did do one thing, though.

"God. Please help me."

It was a simple plea, one I had never made before, even in my most horrific moments. But I did then, and it was sincere. I was acknowledging I had a problem. Even more, I was acknowledging it to Him.

At that moment, the Lord responded, not with an audible voice or a vision of some 50-foot-tall Jesus basking in heaven's light, but with a feeling. A sense. Suddenly, shockingly, I knew in my heart I was going to be okay. I didn't know what that meant or how it looked. All I knew was that it was going to be different from that point forward.

It certainly has been. Today, I'm a Jesus-loving, belly-laughing, friend-hanging, single woman who loves people and animals (in that order; for some, it's the other way around). God has given me the freedom to lead as I fight for and love God's children who feel so broken that giving up appears to be their only option. I do this as a licensed professional counselor anointed to be a conduit of God as the Holy Spirit works through me to help people heal. My typical clients are dealing with dual diagnosis (addiction with mental illness) encompassing co-dependency, adult and childhood sexual trauma, and issues related to abuse.

I've pushed the envelope for the acceptance of dual diagnosis ever since I came into the counseling field over 30 years ago. Most people won't treat addiction and mental illness together, but I always have. After all, I suffered from a dual diagnosis of major depressive disorder and post-traumatic stress disorder. I also had a severe addiction to alcohol and drugs. Incredibly, God has taken the brokenness of my own personal experiences and now uses them for good as I help others navigate their own personal prisons. Another avenue God has used my to help others through my story is the No Limits Women's Conferences, LLC, an organization that exists to bridge the gap between life's struggles for women and spirituality, that I co-founded with Dr. Jana Lovelace (whose story is also featured in this book).

While I know God has healed me, I still deal with the aftereffects from the traumas which shifted my brain chemistry, as I am on an anti-depressant. I talk about these things openly and honestly because God told me many years ago that I was going to be used to educate people to reduce the stigmas that still exist about mental illness. Some see mental illness as a spiritual condition, and to a large degree, it is. Yet there are also many people like me who need to be on medication just like a person with diabetes who needs insulin. That's why we have to be careful within Christianity not to send the wrong message. There are hurting, mentally ill, and addicted people in our midst, and they need our help and acceptance, not our judgment.

As is the case with so many other people, my traumas began early and came often. I was sexually abused as a child by family members, which resulted in me never feeling safe and always feeling alone. To this day, I don't have absolute, concrete memories of the abuse, but I know that it happened. If God ever wants me to experience these repressed memories, He'll allow it. Otherwise, I'm not seeking to draw them out.

————

I was a late baby. My mother, Dorothy, was 42 and my father, Willie, was 50 when I was born in Washington, D.C. I truly adored my parents. They were very good people, and they were devout in their faith. I loved and honored them. My sisters, Mary Virginia and Lois Jean, were 16 and 22 at the time, and the oldest was pregnant at the same time my mother was pregnant with me. Since I was such a late baby, my sisters fought over what I was going to be named. Complete opposites, they both wanted what they wanted, so my parents came up with a compromise incorporating each of their names: Jean Marie.

Lois Jean had a rare and serious curvature of the spine, so she and her family had to move in with us when I was about two. She needed several surgeries, during which two of her ribs had to be removed because of the curvature, and the left side of her body was paralyzed. By all accounts, she should've died on the operating table. But because of her indomitable will and fight, she not only survived, but lived until she was 57. When Lois Jean and her three young boys came to live with us, mom became the primary caregiver for everyone, and it was a full house to say the least. Yet I didn't feel I fit in. In fact, it felt more like I was adopted.

My mom was raised in West Virginia and was the middle of eight children. My dad was the second to the baby of ten children. We were raised in a very orthodox religion. My mother suffered greatly with postpartum depression after I was born. That was where I was introduced to depression. As a small child, I learned not to cry. If I cried, I got hurt more. So, I stopped crying at age three and didn't shed another tear for 30 years, so pent up were my emotions.

My earliest memories were particularly telling. The first was when I was two-and-a-half years old. I was waving goodbye to my mother as she was leaving for work, and I was being watched by Lois Jean and her husband. As I was backing away from the vehicle, I fell into a tree well. I remember bawling and feeling utterly abandoned as I watched my mother's car pull away. Lois's husband got me out of the tree well. The second memory, perhaps when I was three, was of getting my mouth washed out with soap along with Lois Jean's boys. I recall sensing that it wasn't fair, that somehow, I didn't do what I was accused of doing.

I am of the firm belief, because I see it almost every day in my practice, that our earliest childhood memories shape our belief systems, for good or for bad. We carry that into our adulthood. I know I did. As a result of my two early memories, I constantly felt alone and unable to get close to anyone until God healed me from those ingrained feelings.

I started school early, too. I was just five when I entered first grade in Bethesda, Maryland. Perhaps it was because everything was pretty chaotic at home, but I struggled as a student. I didn't read well, and I probably would have been diagnosed with ADHD had it been years later. However, I believe my classroom struggles were an extension of the depression I was experiencing. I went to Catholic school until eighth grade. When my father retired, we moved to

Sanford, North Carolina where I started public school for the first time in high school.

One thing I had going for me at school was that I was a gifted athlete. Both of my parents were coaches and natural athletes themselves, and I definitely had my gifts in that area. I excelled at golf, basketball, and softball. I ran track. I played tennis and volleyball. Before her spinal condition, Lois Jean was also a good athlete. Through her tenacity, she carried on as a basketball and softball coach, and she ended up coaching me. Yet how I looked at myself as an athlete negatively affected me. I believed that my sense of how my parents valued me rested on my athletic ability—so I made athleticism my identity for years to follow. Even after high school, I played basketball and volleyball at the junior college level, and competitive softball into my early thirties.

It's a testament to my physical ability—or a miracle—that I achieved any of that at all considering how much alcohol I was drinking. I had my first drink at age 10. It was from a champagne fountain at a New Year's Eve party my parents hosted, and from then on, I was hooked. I could drink an exorbitant amount of alcohol. That made sense, in that alcoholism ran in my family. It was a generational curse, the kind that progresses from parent to child without skipping a beat. By age 13, I was drinking beer every weekend. By 14, I totaled my boyfriend's car. I was having blackouts. It's funny in a way. There I was, the all-American athlete. The all-American kid. Everybody loved me. But I had this Dr. Jekyll and Mr. Hyde personality when I drank, so I couldn't tell you what I was going to do after I started.

That was the backdrop of my life when I finished junior college at age 19. I started mixing drugs with alcohol because

I thought my athletic career was over. I went into a serious identity crisis which deepened my depression, accelerated my drinking, and foreshadowed one of the single worst moments of my life.

———

Because of my strict religious upbringing, my virginity was important to me. A lot of girls around me were having sex, but I was determined that I was going to stay a virgin until I got married. Even as I struggled with my identity, that desire remained—until it was cruelly and violently taken from me.

During a snowstorm, in a trailer outside of Raleigh, North Carolina, I was raped and beaten by multiple perpetrators to the point that I was unrecognizable and basically left for dead. I suffered two broken ribs, a fractured eye socket, and a broken nose. I still don't recall why I was at the trailer or who precisely was there. I do remember that the first thing I saw when I came to was my blood on the walls and saying to myself, *God, why didn't you allow them to kill me?* If I hadn't been such a survivor, I surely would've have died. After the attack, I stayed holed up in my apartment for the next six months, doing only what I had to do to work and make ends meet until I was fully recovered physically. Emotionally, though, I was as broken as ever. I drank. I shot up methylenedioxyemphetamine or MDA, a psychedelic closely related to Ecstasy. I used cocaine and heroin. I was going into oblivion, and I could've overdosed at any time. I didn't find out the extent of my injuries from the rape until much later, but the moment I felt like I was physically well, I basically went on about my business like nothing ever happened. I buried it, and the people that were around me never talked about it because I wouldn't allow them to do so. My depression deepened.

When the memories of that terrifying day began to return 13 years later, they came slowly in flashbacks, like quick movie clips with no start or end. I remember looking into a mirror and seeing everyone but me. That is called disassociation, and I did it so I could survive. That's very common to trauma. I'd wake up in the middle of the night sitting straight up in bed sweating, and it was like it was happening again, but I never saw me until several months into the flashbacks. Then I realized it *was* me, and it was horrible. Later, though, I got a flashback showing how I fought back against my attackers, and that gave me some comfort. Today, God has healed me. It took a long time, but it is possible to recover from such brutality. There is hope.

Just a few years later, my sister Mary Virginia committed suicide. She was only 41 and had three children and a grandbaby on the way. I was away at a softball tournament when I got the call at midnight. From then on, the drinking continued, but it was no longer fun. I was doing it just so I wouldn't feel anything. It was all I could do to put one foot in front of the other. I was trying to survive. I hid my pain well from others. People would meet me and fall in love with my personality. I was always a practical joker. I loved to laugh. I enjoyed being with people and wanted them to come close, but I was a shell of a person. I couldn't let anybody get too close to me. I couldn't have a healthy relationship with anyone because I was so sick. I was bound up in rage.

I wasn't going to let anyone in, but I couldn't get out, either. I was in my own prison.

Fitting, then, that it was in that jail cell, at age 31 after my third DUI, that I called out to God for help and for the first time felt, inexplicably, that things were going to be okay. Propelled by that tiny act of faith and His response, I was released. I knew from then on that I was going to seek Him, and I pushed myself to get better. I rolled into Alcoholics Anonymous (AA) and began a journey that basically knocked my socks off. I was reintroduced to God. The first day, we talked about surrendering to win. I had never surrendered to anything. I did that. I had to, but I understood that addiction had beat me like a drum. I had to do a mental health assessment and admitted I had a problem, a radical change for someone who had protected her addiction all of her life.

As I continued the AA meetings, I discovered the Lord wasn't all hellfire and brimstone. I learned that He loved me. It was a massive turning point.

My sobriety date is New Year's Eve, 1991—exactly 22 years after that first drink of champagne at my parent's party. Not long after that date, I was officially diagnosed with Major Depressive Disorder and PTSD, and I was able to begin treatment for both. Finally, vocational rehabilitation in North Carolina paid for me to finish my undergraduate studies and even paid for me to get my master's degree.

I'd come a long way, and God had me headed in a positive direction. But there were still more obstacles ahead, challenges that would further define who I am today as a woman and as a leader.

Eight years into my recovery, I was working a very stressful job supervising a great number of people in a 40-bed adolescent addiction facility where I was the clinical director. Remarkably, I was beginning to fulfill the destiny and purpose God had placed within me to help others. Yet my mother was also in very bad health at that time. She had Alzheimer's disease, and I was caring for her at the home we shared in Killen, Alabama while overseeing the addiction facility. It was then that I was diagnosed with Hepatitis C, a consequence of my earlier IV drug use. As I began treatment for the infection, I became severely depressed. Due to treatment, my thyroid no longer functioned. I was so sick I had to take a year off of work while staying with my mother to care for her. It was hard, but I was so thankful to be in a place in my sobriety where I could take care of her and myself.

By the time she passed away, I had recovered and returned to work, and I poured myself into my job in an effort to avoid my own emotional pain. At the same time, though, I began to culminate my search for God that started back in that jail cell. I was raised in a religion where I was christened as an infant. I'd always known about God. After my AA experience, I continued to seek God and came to believe that it was Him who saved me from alcoholism and drug addiction. He even helped me to forgive those who had raped and beaten me, along with those who had abused me as a child. But I still hadn't made the step to enter into full relationship with God. This was my first picture of how He chases after us, even before we are chasing after Him.

In the wake of my mother's death I started going to church—and I was undeniably drawn to Him. In November 2013, I acknowledged Jesus Christ as my Lord and Savior and repented of my sins. Two months later, on January 26, 2014, I was publicly baptized. It was awesome. I was surrounded by very close friends, surrogate family if you will. When I came up out of that water I shouted, "Jesus!" It remains the favorite day of my life.

Then, as I continued to grind away at work, I made an agreement with God that I was going to stay there one more year, help them to find a replacement for me, and open my own private practice. However, near the end of that year, we lost an employee and I decided, without consulting the Lord, that I was going to stay on. God apparently wasn't happy with that. Shortly afterward, my supervisor confronted me and told me that I either needed to resign or be fired. I was so burned out, irritable, and discontented. The Lord slammed that door, I resigned, and on September 15, 2015, I went into private practice as a therapist.

When I began my private practice, I had just refinanced my home and had about $12,000 available that I invested into the launch of the private practice. I did not have a built-in caseload from my previous position, so I had to nurture new clients and began to grow slowly through word-of-mouth and referrals. I barely got by in 2016 and was doing better in 2017 when, in September, I went off of my anti-depressants. I believed God had directed me to stop taking the medication—but the impact on my brain chemistry was profound. I couldn't sleep. I became irritable and discontented. How I felt reminded me of when I began having flashbacks about the rape. It was terrible. At the same time, my clientele decreased dramatically. I was broke. I seriously didn't know where my next meal was coming from.

From then into early 2018, I experienced what I call it the "crushing." It's from the title of a T.D. Jakes book that talks about how God turns pressure into power. In the end, that's certainly what He did for me. I was prideful and truly needed humility. God put me on the potter's wheel and molded me. I needed to surrender to Him and become totally dependent on Him. The pressure of my emotional instability combined with the financial fallout brought a spiritual dependency on God where I was refined, pruned, and, where needed, crushed to be able to step in and do what He has called me to do today with No Limits. Until then, I thought my strength carried me, but I learned that it is only through His strength that I can do anything.

In all, it took about five months to recover from my "crushing." I pressed in and got ready for an overflow. I read and studied my Bible like never before. I began tithing the first 10 percent of everything I earned. I did whatever He told me to do. I also returned to my medication and am not coming off of it again. I don't own my depression, though. As far as I'm concerned, I don't have it as long as I take my medication.

When the breakthrough came in the spring of 2018, I got 20 new clients in a *week*. That simply never happens. Things have remained steady ever since—and I'm now at a place where I absolutely love my life and feel like I'm just hanging around waiting for the next miracle to happen. I continue to deepen my intimate relationship with God, which constantly blows my mind. He allows me to run His business for Him through my therapy practice, Jeannie Lynch, LPC-S, NCC, LLC. He sends me the exact people I need to see. I've always had what feels like instinct when treating clients, but I know it's the Holy Spirit. He tells me stuff during a session. We have it down to an art where there's not even a pause. I'd like to take credit for it because it is so cool, but it is not me. It is Him, and it is awesome.

Through my work with the No Limits Women's Conferences, I'm stepping out of my comfort zone like never before and becoming the leader God wants me to be. I'm leading a women's small group in my church called the Sprouts. In it all, I'm realizing that I am a natural born leader. I didn't know that because my voice had been stolen from me, but over time and through His healing, God has given me back my voice, restored it to health, and called me to be a leader of women. I am convicted that the Lord is calling a lot of women to step out of the boat to exemplify leadership principles of character, authenticity, and servant-heartedness, but *feelings* stop them. We are to follow the truth, not our feelings. That is "God-fidence," where we do not have confidence in ourselves or our own ability alone, but in Him.

Finally, God was the catalyst to my healing. If human beings could do to me what was done to me, I wanted no part of the human race. I was a tough cookie, and I wasn't going to let anyone get close to me. I had to learn God's grace and mercy. It has been tough, but it had to be tough in order for me to comprehend. For myself or anyone who has been through similar traumas and challenges, I can say without any hesitation that anything is possible with God. Don't give up. You can heal and live in *freedom*. You do not have to remain a victim of your past. He will release you from your victim mentality. You can take your thoughts captive to the obedience of Christ (2 Corinthians 10:5), be released from negative thinking about your identity, and become the woman God created you to be. Romans 12:2 declares, "Do not conform to the pattern of this world, but be transformed by the renewing of your mind. Then you will be able to test and approve what God's will is—his good, pleasing and perfect will." That's how you combat mental illness and addictive behaviors.

Through my struggles, the passion and love I now have for Jesus Christ is so worth it. I live each day by choosing joy. There hasn't been a day since that crushing that I haven't felt joy. Why? Because "the Lord is close to the broken-hearted and saves those who are crushed in spirit." (Psalm 34:18) Does that mean life is groovy every moment of every day? No. But I face it with joy. The struggles are teeny tiny in comparison to the joy I have in Him. God has bestowed upon me "a crown of beauty instead of ashes, the oil of joy instead of mourning, and a garment of praise instead of a spirit of despair." (Isaiah 61:3) I am totally dependent on God. In my weakness He is my strength. I am nothing without Him.

All of the events of my life are the pieces of who I really am as a person, and I firmly believe God has used them for my good and the good of others (Romans 8:28). I am able to share my past struggles with others who may be having similar experiences, and the beauty of it is that I can honestly say, "If I can do it, so can you." You can trust Him. He is trustworthy. I can also say, from a place of rawness in my heart, that I have forgiven every single individual who brought me harm. I cannot express to you what that means.

Because of the freedom I have found in Jesus, He has healed the wounds of my past which allows me to be better able to lead others to that same freedom.

This is the freedom to lead.

 Jeannie Lynch has a passion for connecting with people and seeing them improve the quality of their life. She has specific expertise in treating addiction, grief, trauma/ abuse, anxiety, depression, stress management, relationship issues, codependency, ADHD, and other behavioral disorders. She also offers consultation services, diagnostic evaluations, and fit for employment assistance. Contact Jeannie at jlynch-lpc@gmail.com.

2

······

Blazing Trails

Catherine Ripley

AS A CHILD, I told parents nearly every day, "I want to be a professional musician." But they may as well have heard, "I want to join the circus."

In the end, neither of those happened—but what did happen was a series of unexpected adventures and journeys that took me around the world, back again, and eventually back to playing music.

I have never thought of myself as a pioneer. The word always evokes visions of Laura Ingalls Wilder and "Little House on The Prairie." Pioneer women wore kerchiefs and gave birth in cornfields. Still, folks have been using that word for me for a while now, and I'm starting to own it.

I must admit, though, that I prefer "trailblazer" much more. It speaks of adventure and danger. Trailblazers wielded machetes and slashed their way through jungles, flew planes and spaceships around the world, and got appointed to the Supreme Court. Trailblazers are heroes like feminist writer and women's rights advocate Mary Wollstonecraft, aviator Amelia Earhart, explorer Sacagawea, and legendary bass guitarist Carol Kaye.

Well, I own a machete, got lost in Kathmandu, flew in an F-18, contracted malaria in Timbuktu, and worked in five continents. So, yes. Trailblazer it is.

I certainly don't consider myself extraordinary. In fact, someone once said extraordinary people are merely ordinary ones who found themselves in extraordinary situations—and I have certainly found myself leading and being led by countless extraordinary people and in many unusual places. However, growing up as a young girl I had no intentions of leading anyone anywhere, really. My sights were set on being a professional bass player. As all young people do, I was simply trying to find my rhythm, keeping the beat, and discovering a lot of new jams I never knew existed. And so, like the tree that falls in the woods, a musician must share their sound and life lessons, both to be heard and to help someone else find their own voice.

Growing up in the 1970's in tiny, rural Wolf Point, Montana, I could feel the vibrations of a power I couldn't describe being amplified around the world. We were all being carried off by the waves of the civil rights movement, the feminist movement, and the fall from grace in the aftermath of Vietnam and Watergate. Nothing would be the same. The world was no longer black and white—even color television was still pretty new then—and long-standing traditions were being toppled over. I was completely caught up in it in middle and high school. I literally felt the power of the women's movement, which allowed me to stop trying to please society and start pleasing myself. I ran away from the expectations to be pretty and desirable and threw myself at music, politics, sports, and books. I was insatiable. But I was all force and no vector. I wanted to be oceanographer Jacques Cousteau, save the whales, and have my own all-girl rock band.

Little did I know all that would change with the flick of a pen when Congress signed the bill to allow women into the U.S. Naval Academy. That turned my world upside down and, as I'd later discover, right side up.

But that story, like any good one, needs to start at the beginning, and that's with my parents in the 1940's. Back when men wore hats and women wore bright red lipstick, the image I always had of my parents was glamorous and romantic. I pictured their lives being pretty much like an epic World War II movie, the setting being U.S.-occupied Japan: bobby socks and saddle shoes, dance halls, dinner parties, and drives in the country in their big, blue Buick, and picnics where they dreamed and planned their life together. My dad, William "Bill" McGurk, a depression-era Pittsburgh boy, was a U.S. Navy chief petty officer corpsman stationed in Sasebo, Japan. That was where, right after the war ended, he met my mother, Hiroko Miyachi, a beautiful Japanese girl from a large and very traditional family. The lingering aftermath of Pearl Harbor and the devastation of Japan in the war made things obviously problematic for them.Sadly, their life together began with the age-old story of an American sailor marrying a foreign woman and her family disowning her. That was especially common in Japan where the U.S. dropped two atomic bombs on Hiroshima and Nagasaki. Those were fresh realities, and Nagasaki was

19

a mere 40 miles southeast of Sasebo, her hometown. Their lives teach us that everyone has a backstory.

Still, my mother left her family and country to marry my father and move to the United States. She was banished. Her loss and sacrifice are things I can never know, even if her arrival to a foreign and racist country was something I would come to know. Thankfully, she returned home 10 years later with him and her three daughters—me, Vanna, and Christine—and her family forgave her and even gave her a traditional wedding.

I was the oldest of that trio of girls, born in Minneapolis, Minnesota, where we lived for the first few years of my life before my father's retirement from the Navy took us to Gary, Indiana just outside Chicago, Illinois. My early years were quite ethnic, living amongst enclaves of European immigrants where Greek, Italian, and Japanese were spoken in our home and with our friends. My father and his brother were big labor union leaders and promoted local politicians. On weekends, our house was filled with the smell of smoke, whiskey, and perfume and the sound of folks arguing about the steel mills, immigrant workers' rights, and local politics. I soaked it all in through osmosis, and the concept of championing the underdog would later become part of my own quest. I was drawn towards the living room and basement card games, not the kitchen where the wives prepared the meals and drinks. Even then, I was rebelling before my time. I wanted to be in the room where it happened. I wanted to be as powerful and "smart" as a man. It was a different world— and it shows us how children see and hear everything.

My mother, a Japanese immigrant, was stigmatized, as were we, her children. Half-breeds and much more vulgar labels were laid upon us. I learned at a very young age how deep the wounds of racism can cut and scar. So, in what seemed to a 12-year-old to be an overnight decision, my father announced, "Pack your bags. We're moving to Montana." Wolf Point really looked like the end of the earth to us in the badlands close to Canada and North Dakota. My mother cried when we arrived. But my father either knew what he was doing or was simply being led by divine providence, because it ended up being a fairy-tale childhood.

As a salty Navy chief, my father raised his three girls the only way he knew how—like sailors on a ship. So, by default and being five years older than my baby sisters, I was his crew leader. I was the one who mowed the lawn. I was the one who went fishing with him. I was the one he taught how to change tires and hunt for deer. I was the son he never had, yet he also told me, "You can't depend on a man. You have to work hard, go to college, and become a bread winner," adding, "and playing your flute won't do that." (Never mind that I actually played clarinet.) He worked with Admiral Chester W. Nimitz of World War II fame, who always shared with him leadership tips and quips like, "Praise in public and discipline in private." Of course, he laid them all on me. Little did I know I was also learning how to lead.

My father had a bigger than life personality, but it was my mother's understated Japanese culture that came to impact my leadership style more than I ever could imagine. I was struck by her unspoken way of taking on tasks, getting things done, never complaining, never seeking credit, and always, always showing people gratitude, no matter how small the deed. Both of my parents pushed me to excellence, but it was my mother who was the unspoken model

21

of self-discipline, hard work, and generosity. It was also the "B" side of her personality that made her a true enigma as a Japanese woman—she was hilarious. Slapstick Lucille Ball-funny. She once made her Japanese girlfriend laugh so hard that she spit out her dentures and chipped them on the cement. That in turn made them both laugh so hard they wet their pants. She was goofy and completely unselfconscious. In the face of banishment, racism, an atomic bomb, and unimaginable loss, she never lost her sense of humor nor her lightness of being. Her untiring optimism is contagious. *That,* to me, is the definition of courage, and she taught me how your parents or caregivers are your first experience in leadership—good, bad, or ugly.

The first musical instrument I played was indeed the clarinet. It was an arbitrary choice. I picked it not even knowing what it was, but I wanted more than anything to be in the junior high band and be with my girlfriends there. I became proficient with the woodwind, and I quickly developed an interest in jazz and wanted to be in the school's jazz combo, but they didn't need a clarinet player. No one was playing bass guitar, though, so I raised my hand, again not knowing anything about the instrument but confident I could learn to play it well. I believe music is innate in all of us, as natural as your heartbeat. But, my teachers, Mr. Nimmo and Mr. Listerud, who loved their professions and us, pushed us to excellence. A lot of what they taught—discipline, practicing, being part of something bigger than yourself—was really metaphorical. Every part you play, whether small or big, is important and part of the greater whole.

Academics came easily to me, so I sailed through them in order to do as much of everything else that I could to include music and sports. With my two best friends, Katy and Tana, we pretty much blazed our way through the halls of Wolf Point High for four years. I think it was the audacity, confidence, and "the world is ours" attitude that led us to believe we could get away with anything—and we pretty much did. We dressed up in makeshift alien costumes, pantyhose over our faces and blow dryers (laser guns) in our belts to raid teachers' private home parties. We were the three who led the pep rallies, skits, and musical theater productions. Our love of theatrics also led us to the "old folks' home" in Wolf Point where we brought homemade cookies and sang show tunes. That's also where Tana and Katy taught me how to tune out the world, look into the eyes of a lonely stranger, and genuinely listen to and love them. All these years later, the three of us remain close friends and true confidantes. Never forget who you are and from whence you came, and girlfriends are important.

———

In 1976, the U.S. Naval Academy in Annapolis, Maryland ended a nearly 200-year tradition and admitted its first female midshipmen. As I neared graduation in 1978, my parents urged me to apply. I really only wanted to be a music major and had earned scholarships to the University of Nevada-Las Vegas and the University of Kansas. I figured the Navy wouldn't want someone like me, but it turns out they did—and I couldn't say no, in spite of my musical ambitions. So, the first woman from Montana ever to be appointed to the academy and a member of the third class of women to ever enter the academy also became the first woman in the Naval Academy Jazz Band. Music always finds a way.

Annapolis was clearly not ready for women yet. But there we were. Even the uniforms didn't conform. Mine was baggy in the neck, big in the waist, and tight in the hips because it was made for a young man. I was tiny, so my uniform actually had staples in my sleeves and my trousers to help it fit my five-foot, two-inch height because the minimum height requirement for men was two inches taller. While the time-honored tradition of physical hazing had been largely done away with by the time I got there, there was still verbal hazing that I was unprepared to face. The terms "political correctness" and "sexual harassment" weren't even coined in 1978, so nobody really knew how to manage young men and women in that environment. The upper class and officers were used to yelling at young boys, calling them names and humiliating them. Now young girls were being humiliated and yelled at, and it wasn't very pretty.

But as an 18-year-old girl, I didn't know what I didn't know—so I took what I got and learned to adapt as I went. After being written up several times for things like, "Midshipman McGurk rolled her eyes when being questioned by her superiors," I learned to "keep my eyes in the boat" and shut my mouth. It really wasn't too hard. I used to debate with my father on a daily basis, and I knew which battles to fight and which ones to ignore. That feeling was self-imposed to some degree, but the prevalent sense was that I had to prove my worthiness at every turn. I lettered on the sailing team, starred in musical theater productions, and was the only female in the jazz orchestra. Every time I succeeded, I told myself, "Okay, I proved myself. They not only have accepted me, they now know I can actually kick butt." Time and again, it astounded me when later, as a commissioned officer, male colleagues responded incredulously with, "Oh, wow. She really knows her stuff." If a man walked into a room in uniform or a suit, he was automatically given respect as a proven officer. When a woman walked in, all they saw was—well, a woman. Always hold your head up high and you will own the room. A chip on your shoulder is ugly, but kicking butt while smiling is attractive.

Having to prove myself as a woman was neither exhausting nor maddening. I knew the playing field, and I knew how to play my strengths. It isn't fair. It isn't right. But the fact is women do have to give 120 percent in male-dominated organizations when our male counterparts might only need to give 80 percent. Isn't it ironic, then, that the average woman in a comparable position makes 80 cents to the dollar a man makes? There have been improvements, of course, since 1982, but change is slower in some professions than others. So, we chip away at it and do what we can to change our little corners of the world for the better. Wherever there is a minority fighting for justice, equal pay, and equal rights, there must be a concerted, focused effort. While I was at the Naval Academy, there were less than 300 women compared to 4,000 men. That's a significant minority. My roommates and I stuck together, but there was never any type of organized or even underground movement for all of us female midshipmen to come together. That was our mistake. There is always strength in numbers. But we wanted to be integrated. We didn't want to be seen as a gaggle of women or a conspiring minority. We desired to be thought of and looked at as equal, but we didn't have a collective voice.

It has been over 30 years since then, and there remains underlying animosity, sexism, and other -isms at the Naval Academy and in the world. Still, things are a lot better. The #Me Too movement opened the floodgates, allowing all of us to hear the stories of other women and say, "I've felt that, too. I've never been brave enough to say anything, but look at all these other women who are speaking up. I can be part of that greater voice. I am not alone." Embrace and support your sisters. Teach a new generation.

When I took my first division as a leader, I suddenly had power. Not much, but it was still power, so I wielded it. As a 22-year-old division officer, I was unapologetic for my gender, my race, and my size, and those under my purview would be unapologetic, too. So, the quote "think globally, act locally" was always applied to my limited sphere of influence. I didn't change the system, but I controlled my small corner of the world—from Timbuktu to Kathmandu.

―――――

I believe we learn more from failure. Not being afraid to fail actually empowers you to leap without a net, sail without a compass, and dive without scuba gear—all of which I have literally and figuratively done but don't advise. I have led everyone from sailors to engineers to volunteers, and I have learned to be flexible with and discerning about those under my charge. I teach a class on leadership entitled, "Women Leaders: The Hats That We Wear." In every position I've held I've worn several of them: coach, champion, cheerleader, sister, disciplinarian, mentor, and mom. My leadership style has adjusted depending on the demographics: younger or older, sailors or civilians, elderly volunteers or young paid interns. I had to nurture some groups a bit more, while others, especially sailors, responded best when I was clear and direct in my approach. After a while, I got to know each team member and their backgrounds, family lives, and situations. It wasn't required, but it certainly helped if we wanted to be productive. I learned to tap their strengths, tend to their challenges, and celebrate their diversity. Scott, the father of my children and an acting professor, always told me, "Your students will spot insincerity in a second; therefore, you must truly love them. Truly. Love. Them."

Part of adding credibility as a leader is building a toolbox of credentials. I have often found that some of the most talented, wise, and influential people I've met have no formal education or training at all. I know a guitar player who can't read music but can shred every Jimi Hendrix solo ever played, note for note. But in my professions, training and education were vital to understanding the world and how to go forward with advanced technologies and an ever-changing political environment. Therefore, I attended the Navy Postgraduate School in Monterey, California for graduate school, where I studied National Security Affairs and Russian and East European politics. It was just part of the toolbox.

Women are famous for multitasking, so for years I was raising two toddlers and balancing my time as mom, graduate student, musician, and Naval officer. Perhaps it was the combination of youth and living in a less distracting time of no internet and no social media, but my memories of running five miles a day with the dog, raising babies 15 months apart, and leading sailors every day are not filled with the chaos and time management stress I feel today. In fact, it all seemed so easy—or at least very doable. Then again, Candace and Alex were pretty much the most joyful babies on the planet. I used to think that with all the plates I was spinning, God gave me a break by sending down those perfect children, and they always came first. Just as airline attendants exhort to "put the oxygen mask on yourself first," be sure to take care of yourself and your family first.

In Boston, Massachusetts, from 1996-2000, I had the privilege of training over 1,600 midshipmen to receive degrees and commissions from Harvard University, MIT, Boston University, Tufts University, and Northeastern University. It was there I had to apply my own leadership skills to teaching potential officers how to lead and providing them with all the necessary tools to lead others on board ships, aircraft, submarines, and on shore. I took that challenge with an enormous amount of pride as half of my midshipmen were women, and I was one of a handful of military officers in the country at the time to offer what I never had—a female role model. It was a treat to watch over 800 young women graduate and go on to lead a new generation of sailors with the added advantage of learning from at least one female leader. Pass on your lessons learned. Knowledge is not a zero-sum game.

In 2000, I began serving as a U.S. diplomat in The Hague, Netherlands. In the Netherlands, I was the liaison in the office of defense cooperation between the U.S. Department of Defense and the Dutch Navy. We were NATO allies. My family loved every minute of living in Europe—the taste, sounds, smells, and sights of a world much older than ours was enlightening and broadening. Learning new languages and cultures taught my children respect, tolerance, and appreciation of all things foreign. We traveled all over Europe and even took a safari to the Serengeti in Tanzania. Everything in my career leading up to my diplomatic assignments gave me the strength, power, grace, and confidence to hold my own and gain the respect of the predominantly male Dutch teams I worked with in the Netherlands. I was at the embassy on September 11, 2001. Never before or since have I felt such a strong sense of love for my country as I did that tragic day.

In 2004, I sought and attained the position of defense attaché for the U.S. Embassy in Madagascar and the nearby island nations of Comoros, Mauritius, and the Seychelles. Comoros was 100 percent Muslim, and when I first flew in to meet with its first democratically elected president, I was told that, as a female officer, "He is not going to like you. He is not going to respect you. You are going to have a hard time doing any kind of business there." However, after a two-hour lunch at his palace on the ocean, I was treated with the dignity and respect that I was afforded in every other place I went, and I became fast friends with his wife and children. After that first meeting, we went on to collaborate on issues ranging from counterterrorism and piracy to health and humanitarian assistance. To have finally arrived at a place where I wasn't seen as a woman or a female officer but as an American officer in the U.S. Navy was euphoric. Trust that you have the skill and grace to enter any room with anybody.

My last tour in the military was in Hawaii. I was recruited to work at Special Operations Command Pacific, headquarters for counterterrorism for Asia and the Pacific Ocean. Most of the command were elite members of the Navy SEALS, Army Rangers, and the Army 160th Special Operations Aviation

Regiment nicknamed the Night Stalkers. The Navy JAG officer and I were the only women in this command, which had a concentration of the most testosterone-laden group of men in the military. I expected to be greeted with tolerance at best. I was seasoned, older, and wiser, but still thought, *Here I go again. I'm gonna have to spend a month and prove myself to these men because now I'm a forty-something female Navy commander with no combat experience.* On my first day, the guys in the office handed me a giant bag filled with (my size) camouflage uniforms, boots, a Kevlar vest, and a ton of other items I'd need should we get the call to deploy—and that was that. I was one of them. I didn't have to prove anything at all. I led teams into places such as Nepal, Malaysia, and Thailand, and it was an amazing experience. It was second nature for them to assume that if the general recruited me, then I knew what I was doing. Rank never mattered; only experience, intelligence, and critical thinking. These were guys who had laid their lives on the line in Afghanistan, Iraq, Philippines, Syria, Bosnia, Somalia, and places and on missions I can't mention for security reasons. They were humble. They were confident. There was no time for racism, ageism, sexism, or any labels whose only purpose is to diminish and discriminate. They only saw a Naval officer with a different experience and skill set that could help their mission. It was a wonderful way to end my career in the military. It's good to be proven wrong sometimes.

———

After the Navy, my transition to the civilian world was abrupt and blunt. The difference was so much more than

changing from khakis into a business suit. It was the difference between defending our democracy to simply making
money. On my first day at Raytheon, a U.S. defense company,
I walked into an auditorium filled with a sea of blue suited
men and grey hair. My red dress and stilettos stuck out like
a sore thumb. (Hey, I wore uniforms and dungarees for 26
years!) I was charged with opening a new market in Brazil,
which had just discovered offshore oil reserves and needed
surveillance systems and a plan to protect their coastline
and the precious Amazon rainforest. I was the only woman
and person of color in my entire division. I looked for my
team. There was none. So, I created one and jumped right in.
You don't have to fit in. Stand out and shout out.

One day, a senior female executive there pulled me aside
and said, "Nobody cares how hard you work. Nobody cares
how good you are with people, or how smart you are, or
what a good leader and manager you are. All they care about
here is how many missiles you have sold." That was like a
frying pan to the head for me. Still, I stayed until 2015 and
did what I knew best. I threw together teams and picked
my own projects. We had fun. We traveled a lot. I got into
doors previously closed to Americans for decades. But I
was fooling myself. My heart wasn't into selling missiles.
So, when I finally gave Raytheon my two-week notice, I
moved on to the next phase of my life without missing a
beat: teaching political science at Pima Community College
in Tucson. If you don't like your job, change it to fit your own
needs and style—or just leave.

It was at Pima that I realized I needed to pass on my
international and diplomatic knowledge and use my leadership skills to motivate and inspire students not on what to

think, but merely just *to* think. The "why" is really important when I teach. In my course on "Understanding Terrorism" at the end of each lecture, I end with questions like, "Why is this significant? Why do we need to study the Ottoman Empire to understand 9/11?" I go even further back to Socrates, Plato, and Aristotle—and examine why knowledge is important or even why we need a degree. I don't just tell my students what to do, how to do something, or how to think. I ask them why. If there are no bullets flying by your head, take the time to tell your people "why" when giving them direction or orders.

In January 2018, another opportunity I didn't seek took me into yet another new arena of influence. I was asked to run for political office, and when asked to return to public service, I couldn't say no. My campaign focused on fighting for "progressive change" with a platform that highlighted my views on education, health care, civil rights, economic health, and the environment. When asked to identify my "why" in choosing to answer the call to run for state office, I wrote on my campaign website:

"It's not difficult to understand why so many Americans feel hopeless about the future, and even the present: our government seems beyond repair to many of us. The ruthless and often blinding partisan politics inherent in our legislative system has entrenched our leaders to such a degree, they can't even begin to improve our way of life. So, many Americans have simply given up. That's not me. I have hope. And I'm willing to serve, as my record demonstrates. I have spent most of my life serving this country as a Naval officer in the U.S. and abroad. I have had the privilege of seeing and experiencing firsthand a wide spectrum of societies, cultures, and governments. My hands-on involvement in diverse government and civil programs and systems— ranging from humanitarian assistance to national security strategy and decision making—have given me valuable and unique insight and sensibility, which I hope to use in service of this great state where I have chosen to spend the rest of my life."

It was a contested race with four candidates for two seats. I entered the race a year after my competition and still managed to come within a few hundred votes from winning. I was completely new in politics. I'd never run a political campaign before—but I did what my leadership skills told me to do, and that was to build a team. Just as I had done so many times before, I hunkered down and found smart, talented people to oversee everything from communications to finances to speech writing. In the end, I had 19 people on my team while my opponents only had teams of one or two. I brought in more campaign donations than everyone except the incumbent. Within three months, I knocked on over 10,000 doors, got my petition signed within two months, and had triple the amount of signatures I needed. I threw a giant fundraiser with my sister-in-law, Broadway Tony Award winner Alice Ripley, performing to a theater of adoring fans, had team meetings, and appeared at rallies, coffee houses, and schools. My theme was "go big or go home," and I went out big! It was an exhilarating, fulfilling experience. Knocking on doors showed me the gamut of humanity in my city—from the elite white neighborhoods in the north to the poorest immigrant neighborhoods in the south. I looked into the eyes of desperate mothers, the elderly, and the undocumented. People burst into tears when

I spoke to them. I held them. I comforted them. I promised them, win or lose, that I would work to improve our state. My collective and cumulative skills, education, passion, and experiences had to be put to use. Using your leadership skills where they are most needed is immensely fulfilling.

A faction within the local Democratic Party and labor unions seemed impressed by the success of my dark horse campaign and were astonished that I didn't win, so they asked if I'd serve as executive director for the party in Pima County. The party was factionalized, divided, angry, and pretty dysfunctional. I accepted the challenge. I was tasked to reorganize, revamp, and create a positive, welcoming new environment. I shook the place upside down, recruited a team, and dug in. Again, it was what I knew. Form a team. Move forward. Have fun while doing it. In the words of singer-songwriter James Taylor, "The secret of life is enjoying the passage of time."

I have no idea what is next for me. I'm in three local bands, so perhaps it's time to go pro and end up with my original dream? It's never too late! My life has been mercurial, magical, and unpredictable: in a word, blessed. I tell young women who are already leaders or who desire to become one that you will never go wrong if you listen to your heart, find your own rhythm, sing your favorite songs and create new ones—but be anything but ordinary. Trust that you are and always have been more than enough. Women have superpowers; they just usually don't realize it until much later in life. One of those powers is intuition. You will not go wrong, I promise.

Another is your faith. In the darkest of times, I had faith without even knowing it. But it was always there. It doesn't go away. You just forget it's there sometimes. But you'll see it on a billboard, or in a song on the radio, or the face of a stranger. I know I have lost it many times. But how else can I explain the blessed life I've led and my amazing children?

In the book, *The Count of Monte Cristo*, Edmund Dantes says in his prison cell, "I don't believe in God." Abbe Faria replies, "It doesn't matter. He believes in you."

Catherine Ripley has lived and worked in over 80 countries around the world, speaks three languages, and is a retired naval officer and diplomat, adjunct professor, political activist, and musician. Her unique background in leadership began as one of the first women to attend the U.S. Naval Academy and spans a 26-year career including six years in industry, being professor of political science, and serving as executive director of the Pima County Democratic Party in Tucson, Arizona. Contact Catherine at cathyripley@yahoo.com.

3

Masterpiece of Love

Rosalind Longmire

AS A KID, I loved Highlights Magazine. My favorite part was doing the hidden pictures. I enjoyed searching out and finding the objects cleverly concealed within the image, and exulted whenever I discovered all of them, allowing the totality of the photo to be revealed. I couldn't wait for the next issue so that I could do another puzzle.

Perhaps that childhood remembrance is why I can't help but think of my life as a big puzzle—each piece being lovingly sought out by the Master and then put together into a masterpiece created for His purpose. Every part comes together to form a whole and beautiful picture through each gift, grace, and choice given to me by God so that I may continue to show His love to others through the witness of my life.

Of course, being a successful businessperson in my home community of Tucson, Arizona for 18 years before being called into Christian ministry at the church where I grew up is all a part of the puzzle He's completing. The first pieces were assembled as I was raised in the 1960s-70s on the west side of Tucson in the shadow of Sentinel Peak, better known as "A" Mountain for the 160-foot tall, whitewashed block "A" built from basalt rock near its summit. My maternal grandmother, Lena Brown, lived with us and took care of me and my two older sisters, Delma and Marva, while my parents were at work. My mother, Charsie, was a cook and maid for multiple families in northwest Tucson, while Nathaniel, my father, fulfilled a high-security role at Hughes Aircraft Company. They also owned and worked a janitorial business together at night. Therefore, my parents were only home together briefly, in the afternoons after I got home from school. We'd have dinner together on the weekdays and interacted more on weekends. As we got older, my sisters and I were given chores to do, washing the windows of the house, tending to the yard, and cleaning up after our two rabbits and two dogs. I shared a bedroom with my siblings so that my parents had their own and a third was set aside for my grandmother.

It was a great upbringing. We never lacked the things that we needed, but we didn't always get the things we wanted, either. Delma, Marva, and I went to Girl Scouts or Camp Fire Girls, and we spent a lot of time with activities at church. We also had to learn how to fish because my dad loved to get out on the boat and do it, particularly at Patagonia Lake in the mountains south of Tucson. My mother joined us at the lake to fish, but she wouldn't let our father take us hunting.

He did eventually teach us to use firearms, though, when we went target shooting out in the open desert surrounding the city.

———

Being raised by my Grandmother Lena nurtured a great deal of wisdom in my life. It came from her as she taught me to always be myself. She said people would notice me for who I was, not who I tried to be. She loved to cook, as did my mother, so holidays were always special for us as members of our extended family visited. We were a close-knit group. I especially loved my Aunt Dorothy, my mother's sister who lived next door. She played a big part in my life. We called her Aunt Doll. I also learned from others such as church members that I regularly encountered on the week-ends. From them, I learned how to be in a community and how they had care and concern for each other. Our whole neighborhood was really a village. I remember playing in the park with some of the neighborhood children, including my cousins, that my grandmother took care of after school and during the summer. Somebody was always watching out for us. They influenced us, too. We all had to be on our best behavior. It was all very old-fashioned.

For some reason, I gravitated toward the adults. When my mother had her friends over to the house, I'd always take my dolls and play with them behind our sofa near the doorway into the living room, so I could hear what was going on with the grownups. I was curious. They were just having so much fun telling stories, and I wanted to know what they were talking about. I often wondered, *Why am I always with these older people?* It wouldn't be until I was an adult that I realized the wealth of knowledge and mature perspective I gained from all of these people, each insight a piece of God's puzzle for my life. I learned a lot about being helpful from them and from watching the women help each other.

Like most kids, I sometimes played outside. We played kickball and softball, marbles and hopscotch. We climbed trees and chased June bugs. We had to be creative and imaginative because we didn't have a lot of the things that children have now. But I preferred to stay indoors and listen to music on vinyl or 45 records. I was drawn to gospel music by James Cleveland or to anything sung by Aretha Franklin, while my grandmother loved Mahalia Jackson. Aretha had a voice that was so soothing and calming to me. It was beautiful, and listening to her inspired me. My friends thought I was weird because I spent so much time inside with my music instead of outdoors with them, and I guess I was different. That, too, was something I often wondered about until the Lord later showed me how that love for music, and His message proclaimed through it, were just more pieces to my puzzle.

Essential, too, was the example shown to me by Grandmother Lena. She was a very spiritual woman. I heard her praying throughout the day, and she was always quoting Scripture to us, putting it in everyday terms we could understand. Without fail, she had a time of prayer every morning and stopped to read her Bible three times a day. The Word was like a meal to her. She loved to feed on its truth. One of the things she told us was, "I don't care what you do. Somebody is gonna see." Then I looked in the Bible and discovered that there is nowhere we can go where God doesn't see everything. We can't hide from His watchful eye. As Psalm 139:7-12 declares, "Where can I go from your Spirit? Where can I flee from your presence? If I go up to the heavens, you are there; if I make my bed in the depths, you are there. If I rise on the wings of the dawn, if I settle on the far side of the sea, even there your hand will guide me, your right hand will hold me fast. If I say, 'Surely the darkness will hide me and the light become night around me,' even the darkness will not be dark to you; the night will shine like the day, for darkness is as light to you." There is also a passage in Luke 8:17 that says, "For there is nothing hidden that will not be disclosed, and nothing concealed that will not be known or brought out into the open."

Not that I didn't sometimes test the bounds. I remember being 15 and getting ready to go to the shopping mall. Tube tops were popular then, and I was allowed to wear one at home—if there was no one else around or as long as I had a shirt on over it. But whenever I got ready to leave the house, Grandmother Lena said, "Nice ladies don't go out like that. You need to put on another top." Frustrated, I did as I was told, putting a blouse on over the tube top. As soon as I got to the mall with my friends, off came the shirt— but not for long. We ran into one of my aunts. "I know you didn't leave your house like that," she sassed, and I heard my grandmother's voice in my head. *I don't care what you do. Somebody is gonna see.*

Being the youngest, I tended to get away with things like that, and I admit I may have been a bit spoiled. At Easter, for example, I always got two dresses and an Easter basket from my godmother. I think maybe my siblings thought I was spoiled, too, because I didn't have to do as many chores as they did, and I didn't get the same punishments they did for doing the same things, but because my sisters were older, they believed I was overly coddled. I don't think I was coddled at all. Maybe they thought I got into less trouble than they did because I simply spent as much time with my Grandmother Lena as I could. I traveled a lot with her, too. She took all of us on trips to places like California, New Mexico, and Texas. That's where the rest of her family lived. Our parents usually joined us, and we drove most of the time, but the trips to California for two or three weeks in the summer were by train and only with Grandmother Lena.

In general, though, I was a shy kid that mostly kept to myself. I was a good student, but I didn't have a lot of friends throughout elementary and middle school because everyone saw me as being a "holy roller." I wasn't out late at night playing or getting into trouble. I also wasn't interested in some of the things they were doing. It's not like I carried my Bible around or anything, but they knew I went to church. I didn't want them to call me "holy roller" because I thought it was negative. Despite the teasing, I tried to do the right thing and be kind because that's what we were taught to do. It wasn't until high school, after I joined the track team my sophomore year, that I attained a level of popularity. My track coach, Marisella Kitt, was inspirational to me. She told me, "There is something in you that is not like the other girls." A lot of the girls went out smoking, and they were into boys when I wasn't. I wasn't sassy or disrespectful to her, either. Mrs. Kitt told us to keep our heads up high and believe in ourselves. She also helped me to feel better about myself and to realize that I was not so different from everybody else just because of my faith and the fact that I enjoyed some things they didn't. With her influence, I came out of my shell.

That was good—since I was about to embark on the first of two professions that would require me to be more outgoing and relational.

The puzzle was coming together nicely.

————

Upon graduation from high school in 1977, I attended Pima Community College to earn an associate's degree in business administration. I didn't get my degree until 1993, though, because I worked and went to beauty school in between. I worked a variety of jobs, from retail to manufacturing to office administration, and I headed off to Allure Beauty College in the early 1980's. I had an aunt, who I didn't really know that well but was a cosmetologist, sparking my interest. I started doing my dad's hair when jheri curls were popular. I got the box and read how to do it. When somebody in the neighborhood saw his hair and asked who did it for him, it was encouraging. Then my cousin wanted his hair done and others followed. It was my older sister Delma who first suggested I should do it professionally. It was not only something I enjoyed, but I found it to be relaxing and therapeutic.

Once I earned my license from the Arizona State Board of Cosmetology, I worked as an apprentice for Doretta Scales. She was my personal hairstylist, and when I told her I was thinking about going to beauty school, she told me to come work for her. Doretta was working for another salon and preparing to start her own when I started working for her doing paperwork and that kind of thing. When I finished at Allure, I became her assistant in the salon. Doretta was a really nice lady, gifted as a cosmetologist, and loved the Lord, too. In addition to its therapeutic benefits, I enjoyed cosmetology because I love people. I love talking to them and making them feel better about themselves. I am a good listener.

I was in my twenties then, I still attended church, and my faith was growing steadily. I remembered saying when I was 18 that I wasn't going to go to church every Sunday because that's was what I had to do when I lived with my parents. That period of minor rebellion lasted all of a few months before I found myself going back. I think it was a habit, but I also missed it. It was like I had a small empty void within me when I didn't go. Looking back, I can see how a tendency toward church leadership was building within me. Growing up, I was in Sunday School, then I was the Sunday School secretary, and later I taught Sunday School. There was a group for little girls that were missionaries, and we did missionary work. Later, I became an usher. I think I did everything in the church at some point or another, including serving as church secretary and treasurer. In it all, my love for the Lord developed as I sought Him in the Word and, of course, kept listening to gospel music.

I met my husband at the barber shop where I went to get my eyebrows done. He was 19 years older than me, but he was easy to talk to, a good listener, and a nice man. Pleasant, mild mannered, and low key, it was at the barber shop where I really got to know him better. We dated on and off for about 10 years before we got married, and I wouldn't call it courtship. It was more of a friendship. He had a lot of wisdom, but I had to pull it out of him. We had similar interests. I can't even describe how we fell in love. I just knew. It just kind of happened. We got married in 1995, and I had my first son, Pierce, one year later. Al had two daughters from his previous marriage that were already grown, and we had our second son together, Jarrett, in 2000.

Before my business partner Doretta got married, we closed our shop, and I went to work for a few other salons before Al and I went into business together with a combo barber shop/beauty salon. By then, we had already been married for about three years. The shop was called Al's Barber Shop and Hair by Roz. Funny thing was I didn't see him much during the day. The salon was in the back of the barber shop, and I had a separate entrance. But that was okay with me. There was way too much testosterone going on in the barber shop. I didn't see Al unless I was going to the office or to the restroom. We were so busy—and stayed that way for much of the 18 years we owned the business.

It was great being a businessperson, and I learned three important principles along the way. First, honor God first in all your business endeavors, focusing on customer service. Truly listen to the heart of what they are saying, and treat them well. My clients would converse with me, and I spoke to their soul while I was doing their hair. They shared so many things, and my spirit of discernment was heightened so I could see things, and sometimes when I touched them, I could feel things. Even if they didn't ask, I prayed for them without them knowing about it. Second, believe that you will succeed in your business because if you don't, you won't. Sometimes you get caught up in competition.

When that happened to me, I always went back to what my Grandmother Lena told me: "Be true to yourself."

Finally, be sure to find a balance between your personal and professional life. I had to learn that the hard way. We worked 10, 12, sometimes 14 hours a day. My parents worked hard and long, and I repeated the same trend. The boys, therefore, were with my parents or someone else, but I knew they needed at least one of their parents to take them to play basketball, to karate, or to school plays. Pierce was about nine years old when I finally started cutting back on my hours to spend a little more time with the boys. I wish I had done that sooner and for longer.

I'm still an independent contractor today, working about 20-25 hours over three days each week. I don't work on Saturdays, though, because I'm now using that time to prep for my second profession—if that's truly the correct term for being a pastor.

———

I had been in Phillips Chapel CME Church my entire life. It was my family's church. I grew up there. In 2004, I started studying the Bible more frequently, praying more often, and developing a closer relationship with God. One evening, the house was completely quiet, and I had just finished laundry and had gone to the bedroom to lie down. It was about 11:00 p.m. I dozed off, but I was a light sleeper.

Then, at about two or three in the morning, I heard my name being called. I groggily thought, *Who would be calling me at three in the morning?* Everyone else was asleep.

Quite suddenly, I discerned that it was the actual voice of almighty God.

I took a deep breath.

"Rosalind," He said.

"Yes, Lord?" I asked quietly, reverently.

"Go and read Isaiah chapter six. Will you go for me?"

"Yes, I will go."

I kept a Bible beside my bed. I grabbed it and went into our home office to read so that I wouldn't wake Al. I read the chapter, knowing already that it was the passage where God called Isaiah to become a prophet for Him. In it, Isaiah saw a vision of the Lord seated on His throne with seraphim, the highest level of angels, positioned above Him. They were calling to one another, "Holy, holy, holy is the Lord Almighty; the whole earth is full of his glory," and the sound of their voices shook the thresholds of the holy temple. One of the seraphim flew over to Isaiah with a hot coal in his hand, taken with tongs from the altar. With it, he touched Isaiah's mouth and said, "See, this has touched your lips; your guilt is taken away and your sin atoned for." Then Isaiah heard God say, "Whom shall I send? And who will go for us?" Isaiah responded, "Here am I. Send me!"

It must've been a magnificent sight. I read it two or three times and then started to pray. I was seeking clarity and wrestled back and forth. *Lord, are you calling me to do something? Are you sure you've got the right person?* After a while, I was finally able to lay down and go back to sleep.

The next day, I went in to work like usual. When I'm styling someone's hair, I use hot Marcel irons and the stove that goes with them. They have handles and a little lip on it that closes, and the iron part is placed into the stove to heat them up. A client came in, and as I began styling her hair, I told her about what I had read the night before in Isaiah 6. As I did, I turned my head to smell the hot iron. It's a technique used to determine the temperature. Suddenly, my hand slipped and the iron touched my lips—but it did not burn. It did not blister. It was the most amazing thing!

I looked in the mirror. "Wow! That is God!" I thought of Isaiah's words after he was touched by the hot coal held by the seraphim: "Here I am. Send me!"

And I knew. It was my call to ministry.

That was in 2005. After I was ordained three years later, I went to work under my pastor, serving for two years before becoming pastor of Phillips Chapel in 2010.

When I became pastor, some of the longtime congregants looked at me as still being the same little girl that was raised there. They challenged me on my decisions about the vision of the church, which way we would move, or things I felt we had to do in the church. Others had a problem with me because I did not go to seminary or have a bachelor's degree. It was hard, but the Lord used it to help me realize that I was equipped by the Holy Spirit, not by people, to be the pastor of Phillips Chapel. I had been designed by God to do what He had called me to do. For a while, I had to constantly reaffirm that truth in my heart and display it in my mind and spirit. I had to persevere. I had to hold my tongue. I had to prioritize my time with the Lord in study and prayer more than ever. But once I accepted the truth and legitimacy of my calling, people started coming around. Some didn't stay, but other new people came. The congregation began to embrace who I was as pastor and follow the leadership that God had given me.

I also realized my total dependence on God and not myself. When I first got into ministry, I was the pastor of the church, so I was a vessel to help guide the church. Leading God's people and wanting to do right by Him was very important to me. I never wanted to lead anyone down the wrong path. I didn't want to hurt anybody, and I didn't want to do anything against God. I thought the church was mine to lead—but I gradually began to see it was not mine at all. As my faith grew, I realized Phillips Chapel was His to lead. My dependence needed to be on Him, not on my own abilities. God showed me that I was working with a diverse group of people, and they were His people. All He needed me to do was just love them.

And so I have. Today, I am known as "the pastor of love." My very first sermon, from John 4, was based on love. How do we know that we are loved by God? It is unconditional. No matter what we do, God still loves us. No matter what anybody else does to us, God still loves us. No matter what we do to someone else, God still loves us. His forgiveness and grace are boundless. Maybe that's why people tell me that "I just love everybody." I do. It doesn't matter. I may not like their ways or their behavior, but I still love the person. I first saw and learned unconditional love from my grandmother. When the neighborhood kids got in trouble, she just loved them. God loves His great creation, and He wants us to be better.

———

My greatest passion in life is to see other people experience the love of God. My greatest success in ministry came seven years ago when I met a young, homeless woman who had been in an abusive relationship. She worked with my nephew at Sears and was living in a shelter with her young son. She had nothing. We took her in at Phillips Chapel, and the whole congregation helped her along. She got an apartment. We helped her get furniture. We helped her with her son. He was about four or five at that time, and we provided him with surrogate fathers, men in the church who became father figures to him because he didn't have one in his life.

Today, she has her own home. She is married. She has a happy family. To see how God used me and the congregation to help her come from that broken place to experiencing the love of God was amazing.

It was love in demonstration—and demonstration of love is what God wants from each one of us.

God has developed within me the characteristics to be "the pastor of love" and to show His love to others. The Lord continues to pour knowledge, wisdom, and understanding into me, and He continues to use me to touch the lives of people. As He does this, the puzzle of my life gets more beautiful. The experiences become deeper—and I stand confident that God will continue to bring the pieces together so that, in the end, it's image will be fully reflective of my name.

Rosalind. A beautiful rose.

He'll do the same for you. God created you in His image. As you trust in Him and continue to develop your relationship with Him, the Lord will pour into you the knowledge, wisdom, and understanding of His Word that you need to succeed and lead. He will also position you to touch the lives of others in incredible ways—and become His masterpiece of love for all to see.

Rosalind Longmire is pastor of Phillips Chapel CME Church, the church where she has served all of her life, and she is also a licensed cosmetologist. Her heart's desire is to allow God to use her to build His Kingdom through loving, serving others, teaching, and preaching the Gospel of Jesus Christ. Contact Rosalind at rozlong52@aol.com

4

······················

Waiting to Emerge

Dr. Amanda H. Goodson

THE FIRST THING I saw on the television was a shot from inside mission control at the Johnson Space Center in Houston.

It was a familiar scene. I'd been there before, even if most of my time was spent further east at NASA's Marshall Space Flight Center in Huntsville, Alabama. That's where I worked as Director of Safety and Mission Assurance, the first African American woman to ever hold that position at NASA.

My team and I oversaw mission assurance of the propulsion systems for the Space Shuttle program with direct responsibility for launches. We weren't involved with reentry or landings.

Yet what had me watching the TV that morning on February 1, 2003, the day STS-107, the Space Shuttle Columbia, was scheduled to land, was a phone call from my mother, Mable.

I'll never forget what she said.

"I think the shuttle exploded."

Adrenaline surged through my body, my heart drummed in my chest, and my stomach sank. "No way," I said. "Not on my watch. It couldn't."

Mom's voice was cautious yet gentle. "Please watch, Amanda. I think you'll see." In my shock I didn't respond, unable to even form a word. "It'll be alright, no matter what," she added. "Keep your head up. I know you'll do the right thing."

Perhaps, but at that moment the only thing I could do was stare at the screen as CNN Headline News showed a dark blue sky punctuated by a glowing light with a vapor trail. It looked like a massive shooting star moving swiftly from the top of the screen to the bottom with a slight right to left angle.

"This video was shot when a loud explosion was heard over Texas," the news anchor reported, her voice professional but noticeably shaky. "It would appear there's been a catastrophic incident over the skies of Texas. We are seeing huge pieces of metal reentering Earth's atmosphere."

It wasn't the first time I'd dealt with disaster. I was a young engineer at Marshall back in 1986 when the Space Shuttle Challenger disintegrated in a massive fireball, and was placed by then-Director of Quality Assurance, Wiley Bunn, as deputy lead on a sub-team that focused exclusively on evaluation of the solid rocket booster O-rings to be used on future shuttle missions. I knew what it was like to deal with a mission tragedy, and the lives lost in the process, and come out on the other side.

But this was different. I'd met Columbia commander, Rick Husband, two years before the fateful flight, told him I was one of the people who worked to get him and his crew into space and back safely, and had assured him, "The first eight-and-a-half minutes after launch, I got you," It wasn't a cocky statement, but one born from confidence in myself and the ability of my team.

Now, as it hit me that he and his entire crew were gone, along with the machine that carried them, I wondered what was next for NASA. For the nation.

For me.

―――――

The rest of that story, told in detail in my book *Astronomical Leadership*, saw all of us at Marshall and throughout the entire NASA family come together, investigate the accident, and do the hard, thorough work to ensure a return to flight for the shuttle program in July 2005. The final space shuttle mission took place six years later.

By then, though, I had not only left NASA, but had moved across the country to Tucson, Arizona, had taken on new leadership roles at a major U.S. defense contractor and industrial corporation, and had even become a church pastor. Today, I'm still doing both. I also have a speaking and coaching service, and I have launched a publishing imprint that included the production of this very book.

Through it all, I have learned a lot about myself, my faith, and my leadership—and I have emerged, making an impact in the lives of others in ways I never thought possible.

It's been an unlikely journey, one that began when I was a little girl in Decatur, Alabama in the 1960s. Born to Mable and Harold Harris, I wasn't aware that my father, who was a Colonel in the United States Army, was able to serve because of President Harry Truman's executive order in 1948 ending discrimination in the Armed Services. I barely remember our brief move to California because of my father's military duties before returning home to Alabama in time to see my baby sister, Yolanda, born and for me to start school. I was brought up in a time of significant social upheaval in our nation, and for my family as African Americans. My toddler years witnessed the March on Washington and Dr. Martin Luther King Jr.'s "I Have a Dream" speech and watched the signing of the Civil Rights Act by President Lyndon B. Johnson, preventing employment discrimination. Unfortunately, though, it also saw the bombing at the Baptist church in Birmingham, the police attack on marchers crossing the bridge at Selma, and the assassination of Malcolm X.

I started first grade when I was five and, at my parent's insistence, attended a newly-integrated school a few miles away from home instead of the still-segregated school just one street over. They felt I was going to have more opportunity at the integrated school, and while there were some other blacks there, it was predominantly white. I was nervous and scared at first because I didn't know what to expect, but I learned to adapt despite my uncertainty. I was kind of unique, a laid-back kid, chunky, and a little weird because I processed things differently than others. I was an analytical thinker who needed everything wrapped up in a nice package. Spontaneity didn't come easily to me. I enjoyed being part of the crowd with the other kids, yet I was never really part of the crowd because I was unsure of myself. I was often with people who stretched the boundaries, but I mostly stayed within the rules.

Away from school, as a little girl, I loved to sing. I was in the Sunbeam Band in our congregation at St. James Cumberland

Presbyterian Church. It was a choir with Christian Youth Fellowship that went to other churches or events around town. At home, I sang along to TV show themes and commercial jingles. Mom worked until dad graduated from college when I was three, and then she stayed at home after that, meaning we saw each other much more than I saw my father. As a couple, my parents were quite a pair. While their relationship was centered around me and Yolanda, I could tell that they loved each other. They laughed a lot, played card games with one another, and enjoyed hanging out as a couple with their friends. My parents drove me in different ways. Dad wanted me to learn, read, and succeed. Mom wanted me to be more disciplined in my thinking. She always told me, "You're going to have to be two times better than everyone else, smarter than everyone else, and do more than everyone else because they're not going to treat you the same because of how you look."

For much of my young life, I struggled with self-confidence. In school, my teachers did not think I was as intelligent as the other kids, and in my eyes, the color of my skin certainly played into that perception. I didn't perform well on standardized tests. Still, I made better than average grades in all my courses, even if my teachers didn't recognize it. In addition, I just didn't feel like I fit in at school, so I didn't like it much. I felt shunned by some of the kids. I was teased because of my weight, and I was tall for my age, too. I had only a few friends. By the time I hit middle school in the early 1970s, social progress had surely been made, but segregation and racism were still a part of everyday life in Decatur. Being called racial slurs out in the community was commonplace. When we eventually moved to a house in a better, all-white neighborhood—the first black family to do so in that area—someone burned something on our front lawn. We didn't know for sure what it was, but it left a big brown spot in the thick green grass.

As a high school student, I took part in a math competition and won eighth place in the entire school, the only girl and African American in the top ten. Yet I was shocked when my name was called because I never viewed myself as being smart. Everyone had told me I was average, especially my teachers, and that seeped away my confidence. I never actively sought to be the best I could be. I did try hard in math, and I played clarinet in the marching band, bass clarinet in the concert band, and piano in the jazz band. Yet even there, whenever the jazz director pointed over to me to do an improvisational solo during a song, I couldn't do it. I didn't have the self-assurance to try. I was told I wouldn't be successful in life because my grades were average, and I operated in that assumption. Yet the weight of that expectation, and the nagging self-doubt it created, kept me down.

As my senior year neared an end, I realized I needed to decide what I was going to do as an adult. With my father's encouragement, I went to the library to research what professions paid well that might fit with my two interests, math and music. It was clear. Engineers and accountants generally made money while musicians didn't. So, I thought, *I'll take engineering.* I then made an appointment with a high school counselor.

"Girls are not engineers," I was told, point blank. "Maybe you should go into the military or be a nurse."

That was my first experience with gender bias—and I didn't listen to it. It wasn't that I thought there was anything wrong with being a nurse or in the military. It's just I knew those weren't the paths for me.

So, despite my counselor's advice to not go to a traditional four-year college, I decided I would, starting with Preface, a summer pre-engineering program for high school graduates at Tuskegee University, the school my dad had attended. It was there where my instructors first told me that I was smart. That inspired me to apply myself and study like I never had before. I got results, too, along with more encouragement from my professors. They lifted me to new heights.

Then, from that lofty vantage point, I looked around and saw other students who were doing what I had been doing earlier, and thought to myself, *Wow. This is what 'average' looks like.* From that moment on, I decided I was not going to be average and decided to excel as a young engineering student at Tuskegee—a decision that ultimately landed me with my first post-graduation job at NASA.

I made a choice to not allow my circumstances, grades, or other people to cause drag and weight that would define me and keep me grounded. I discovered that I could do whatever I set my mind to do.

Through Tuskegee's job placement assistance, I had no less than four employment offers waiting for me upon graduation. Two were with Hughes and with the U.S. Air Force, both in Los Angeles. The third was with the U.S. Army in Huntsville. The one I chose, though, was NASA. Not only was it also close to home in Huntsville at the Marshall

Space Flight Center—but it was *NASA!* I'd always thought of our nation's space program as this amazing place filled with smart, cool people. I was hired on June 6, 1983 as a professional engineering intern in the test and evaluation branch. It paid an annual salary of $21,500, which was cool, even though I knew friends from college who were making more with other non-government employers. Nevertheless, I was an engineer, and that was all that mattered.

On my first day at Marshall, I went to the test evaluation branch group to fill out mounds of paperwork, then went to the high bay area where I was given a tour with different people showing me the various departments where I was going to work. I was the first African American *and* first woman engineer in that group, so I got some funny looks, but most everyone was polite and professional. The fact that I was the first engineer there of my race and gender was significant to me, and it created an inner tension that brought back mom's words from my youth about having to be better and smarter than everyone else.

I worked hard through my first year, seeing NASA as my proving ground and embracing my work with gusto. I took part in one interesting project after another. Among them was an isoelectric focusing experiment to be used on the space shuttle. It was designed to take all the constituents of human blood, separate the white and red blood cells, freeze them in a vacuum, and then return them to Earth so doctors could use them for research. I was chosen to represent quality and mission assurance on the project and report back to its director, Wiley Bunn, as the project progressed. He called me in one afternoon to give him the latest update on the experiment. It wasn't the first time I'd been in his office, but I was still taken aback by the sheer size of it. I could do several cartwheels and backflips and not even come close to hitting a wall or ceiling. I guess the space was fitting for one holding his position: Director of Quality Assurance, to be expanded later to Safety and Mission Assurance.

I sat down across from him at the massive conference table. He took a puff from his pipe.

"What do you want to do?" he asked.

"What do you mean?"

"I mean, what do you really want—here at NASA?"

I thought about it and heard a voice within exhort me. *Be bold.*

I leaned forward in my chair. "I want your job."

He blew out a billow of smoke and laughed as if he were thinking I had no idea what I was asking.

"You want my job?"

"Yes, sir!"

He swiveled in his chair and looked straight ahead, as though assessing me as much as his response. His gaze wasn't skeptical, though. It was credulous. Respectful.

"I want to take you seriously," he said. "As a kid, I was taught to throw rocks at black people. I knew that wasn't right." Another puff on the pipe. "I've been looking for someone to help, to create a legacy." He paused. "Okay. If you want my job, you're gonna have to work hard, do the jobs you never want to do, and do the jobs others are not willing to do."

Suddenly, I was the one challenged to take him seriously. Was he really going to give me the chance to go after his position? "I can do all those things."

He got up from his chair, and I rose from mine. "All right,

then. I've got some work to do to make this happen. And no complaining from you, okay?"

"Yes, sir."

I returned to my cubicle, sat down at my desk, and pulled out my engineering notebook. I then wrote down some goals related to what could happen if I had Wiley's job. *I got into engineering to lead, to influence people,* I reminded myself. *This will let me do exactly that!* The pen just flew across the page, I was so enthused. I began to dream about what could be.

True to his word, Wiley started giving me projects. Some of them I didn't like and indeed probably wouldn't have chosen to do. Basically, whatever Wiley told me to do, I did it without question. With each assignment, he wanted me to show him my findings and share my perspectives. He always asked, "Why did you do it that way?" or "How could you have done that better?" Because of the commitment I made to him, Wiley never held back. I wanted his job? He was doing everything he could to prepare and position me to have it. When Wiley was away from his office, I even started going in there, alone, imagining myself in his job, creating a future in my mind.

Calling those things that be not as though they were, waiting for them to emerge.

———

Shortly afterward, in January 1986, the Challenger disaster happened, Wiley appointed me as deputy lead on the sub-team evaluating the solid rocket booster O-rings, and my career at NASA progressed. New assignments, including a year in California, further developed my engineering skills and expertise as a leader, and I became GS15 Director of Systems, Safety, and Reliability at Marshall. At the same time, Wiley had become ill and had to retire. Not long after, Wiley passed away from lung cancer. Without his presence, my biggest sponsor was gone, but he had equipped and prepared me so well that I knew I was ready to move forward without him. He had given me all the experience and exposure I needed, as had so many other key individuals who rallied behind me and supported me—but now it was up to me to take it from there.

I did. In 1997, I was promoted to SES Director of Safety and Mission Assurance—the *very* position Wiley once held. After that, I was wed to Lonnie Goodson and became pregnant with our son Jelonni less than a year later. When my pregnancy leave was over, I tried to find a balance between being a nurturing wife and mother at home and an effective, focused leader at work. At the same time, my desire to progress professionally took a next step as I decided to pursue a doctorate degree. I began school to get a doctorate in church administration, figuring it was going to profit me not just in my NASA duties but also at church by helping me enable degreed people to interact and serve efficiently with others who hadn't completed high school.

My studies also had an unexpected benefit: I studied the Bible more and learned more about it than I ever had in my life. As I did, I thought, *This is pretty cool!* The leaders I learned about from the Bible had such faith and a veracity for life, and they provided lessons I could immediately apply to what I already knew about leadership. I completed the doctorate in 2001 and was even ordained as a minister.

There were no less than 16 different shuttle launches from the time I took over Wiley's old job in 1997 until the dawn of the new millennium. There were exactly 16 more from then until the launch of Columbia in January 2003. Each one had its own set of goals and challenges, and each one added to my skill set as a leader. However, the Columbia disaster in February 2003 ended up being my last space shuttle mission. The personal trauma that followed it, combined with everything I was doing at home trying to be a superwoman wife and mother, wore on me. I couldn't help it. I strived to do everything at peak efficiency because that's how I was wired. I refused to settle for anything less than my best, and my best was probably almost always more than was required.

God knew all that, of course, and orchestrated the move to Tucson in the summer of 2003 that led me into a new and challenging engineering position—and something else utterly unexpected. I dove into church work as I never had before. We attended Tucson's Phillips Chapel CME, a Christian Methodist Episcopal church. Because I had been ordained as a minister, prior to leaving Alabama, to provide the added credibility needed to my doctorate to allow me to officially serve in church settings, I was sometimes asked to be the speaker for services at Phillips. I didn't really see it as preaching, though I suppose that's what I was doing. I had no interest whatsoever in becoming a pastor.

I did lead a women's ministry through the church called "Never the Same" that ended up doing full conference and workshop events in Arizona, New Mexico, Texas, and Alabama. It was a non-profit organization dedicated to reaching women living in mid-sized cities such as Tucson and teaching them about leadership principles within the Christian church. I oversaw a team of ten people, and we brought in keynote speakers and area talent to perform or lead worship. I loved the work. I also sang in the choir at Phillips Chapel and played the piano occasionally. I grew in my love of Bible study and prayer, and I was thrilled at how God strengthened me spiritually through both.

Actually, that had started back before I left Alabama when God led me and my family to come to Tucson. It was then He told me, "I am going to ask you to do something in 2007 that is going to be the most beautiful thing you could do for me." I remember writing it down and figuring it was going to be something big, where I'd be traveling, maybe worldwide. My thoughts were grandiose, but I had no more detail than that. By the time 2006 rolled around, I felt as settled in as ever at work and engaged spiritually at Phillips Chapel. I'd also begun some relationships at Trinity Temple CME, a sister church that we often visited as a congregation for church anniversaries and other special programs, including with Trinity's pastor, Leotis Barnett. A few months later, the Lord prompted me to leave Phillips and begin attending Trinity, where I was eventually given the opportunity to read Scripture or lead prayers as part of the services. Trinity had all of seven people regularly attending Sunday services and had seen no less than five pastors come and go in recent years. I discerned that it needed stability and decided I was going to be loyal, fiercely so, to Pastor Barnett. I also felt led of the Lord to truly humble myself under his leadership, to do whatever he asked, and to champion him to others in the congregation.

In December 2006, I got a call from Pastor Barnett, telling

me he was sick and at the ER. Lonnie and I saw him at the hospital where they were working to regulate his blood sugar. When I looked into his eyes, they didn't look right. He repeatedly asked for water. He also told us then that they were going to keep him overnight to lance a boil on his foot. The next day, Pastor Barnett almost died. During the procedure on his foot he apparently went into shock and had the first of what ended up being a series of strokes. Pastor Barnett then went into a coma. It was the end of the year, and I was on holiday vacation from work, so I visited him every day. I'd talk to him and tell him to wake up, that Trinity needed him. I prayed for him and spoke Scripture over him. But he remained unconscious.

Early in 2007, the CME bishop asked me to take over Sunday services at Trinity. Obediently, I preached every Sunday and remained fiercely loyal to my pastor, just as God had directed me. After seven months, Pastor Barnett finally woke up—but he was never the same again. After the combination of the strokes and coma, he never returned to his right mind. I'll never forget that day, though.

"G-g-g-g-Goodson?" he said, looking at me as I stood over his bed. "That you?"

"Yes, it is."

"Who's pastor at Trinity?"

I wasn't surprised that was his first question. The church was everything to him. I told him who it was because the change had been made a month earlier, but I don't believe the name ever registered in his mind—even though the name was mine.

I was appointed pastor of Trinity Temple CME in June 2007, doing the "most beautiful thing" the Lord had for me in the most unlikely way I could imagine—and I remain there today.

————

In the many transitions of my professional life, from NASA to working with Department of Defense contractors, other business ventures, and even church ministry, I have discovered how important it is to develop the intellectual capacity to help individuals and teams come together to achieve a common mission. I believe everyone has a strategic genius for their particular area that emerges as they learn and work hard to make what they do succeed. The adaptability and ability to revector, reshape, and reinvent yourself is paramount to growing as a leader and overcoming any challenges that come your way.

It's when you go through difficulties and face obstacles that you discover what *not* to do and go in a different direction. If I didn't leverage my challenges, I'd still be going down the same path. Because I had challenges, I was able to take that fork in the road and go in a different direction. You are going to have struggles and setbacks. Use them as a steppingstone to dictate your future. People will always have an opinion about what you *can't* do, but they don't really know what you can and can't do. When someone tells me I can't, that's an indicator of what I *can* do.

Another key to success as a leader is to put the spotlight on someone else. You are on the right course when you are showing others the way and helping them be successful. Whenever you can, position yourself to be a leader and mentor. You'll have an incredible impact. One of my favorite mentors was the late Myles Munroe. His teachings show you how to see yourself as God sees you—as a king of sorts, having authority and yet still being humble as a servant. He also shows you how to create harmony with who you are purposed to be, who you are now, and how both make an impression on eternity even though you are just a little piece of it. Another leader and mentor, Alabama pastor Laura Thompson, taught me self-confidence and self-assurance without being selfish. Others, such as Bishop Jackie Green and Bishop Bobby Best, educated me about leadership in the Christian church and how that can extend into the community. Finally, life coach Anthony Robbins taught me much about neurolinguistics, how the brain works and the relationship between language and the structure and function of the brain, while neuro doctor Caroline Leaf gave me insights on how to reprogram my thinking to get certain outcomes. I have married those perspectives with the truth of God's Word, and it gives me a lot of strength knowing that I can engage my brain in a positive way.

Who are the leaders or mentors in your life? What have they taught you? What can you teach others as a leader or mentor to influence them? You can be at the top of the organization, an emerging leader, or somewhere in-between. You may be in a place where you support other leaders. Regardless of your position, you can still lead from there and influence others in a way that is needed and noted. As a pastor, for example, I've found that I influence others in a significant way by introducing them to the Lord so they can get closer to God and function like He wants them to function. My ability to influence has had to expand itself far beyond what I anticipated. A church congregation includes people of different classifications, skills, backgrounds, and needs. Some learn differently and quicker than others, so you've got to reach each person where they're at, and be that beam of light, that ray of hope, for them.

You also have the ability to encourage others to be their best in a way that positively touches their brain and their heart. It's an enormous challenge but an incredible privilege. In addition, also remember to have the courage to stay out of step when others are marching to the wrong song. Discern where you or the organization needs to go, and if someone else is not following that path, be willing to be different and stay the correct course. Be committed and accountable to the mission. Finally, be resilient and adaptable, pliable in any situation. All of these traits will enable you to defy gravity and rise to a new normal, and others around you will see that and be inspired to raise themselves to a higher place of achievement and opportunity.

In the end, my greatest achievement was to do the "most beautiful thing" as God directed. My biggest opportunity is to learn to listen more quickly to Him. I know that God takes me round by round and teaches and matures me over time, but I wish I had come to know Him more clearly and strongly faster, giving my all to Him in a more expedient way. That way I would have treated His people better, treated His things better, and enjoyed the process more.

As I see myself unfold and God continue His purposes through me, I imagine a butterfly, newly transformed as it emerges from its cocoon, looking at the different colors and designs on its wings as it flutters into the sky, thinking, *Wow! I didn't know I was going to end up looking like this. I didn't know I would have all these hues and shapes. How beautiful! I am so grateful my maker made me like this because I am radiant, different, noticed, and needed.*

That's how I feel about myself—and want you to feel about yourself as well. You possess the capacity and competence to make things happen in a way that will transform who you are, what you do, and the people you touch in an awesome way. You have so much promise inside of you. It just needs to be stirred up, raised up, and unleashed.

It is just waiting to emerge.

Dr. Amanda Goodson is owner and founder of Amanda Goodson Global, LLC, and has over 25 years of experience supporting government agencies, corporate industry, and academia as a leadership strategist, professional coach and consultant, workshop facilitator, and keynote speaker for leaders as well as for churches and faith-based groups. She is a former NASA senior executive, currently a senior leader for a major defense contractor in Tucson, Arizona, and pastor at Trinity Temple CME Church in Tucson, Arizona. Contact Amanda at amandagoodsonglobal@gmail.com.

5

All the Right Situations

Jana Monroe

WHETHER IT WAS through my investigations of everything from missing fugitives and kidnappings to violent crimes, or my work in counterterrorism, counterintelligence, and cybersecurity, my career has certainly been exciting and seen its share of firsts as a female leader.

Yet I've never really felt like I was fulfilling a pioneering role as a woman. Instead, I see my achievements more as simply being in the right situations. I knew I could do the work. It wasn't like I was trying to be a weightlifter or a ballerina or an opera singer, something totally out of my skill set. I was always very comfortable and confident in my abilities.

Perhaps that came in part from my passion for law enforcement, birthed when I first became aware of how

71

much I appreciated living in the United States. I was 13 and a bit of a bookworm. As I read, studied, and learned about our country, I discovered that I loved how we are a nation of liberties and laws. I also hated bullies. I couldn't stand people who took advantage of others. So, I thought, *How can I serve those two callings?* It seemed to me that law enforcement was the way to do it.

My upbringing was also instrumental. As an only child of parents who were also only children, independence was practically a birthright. Born and raised in Long Beach, California, my parents were both from a town that hardly anyone has ever heard of, St. Edward, Nebraska. When I was seven, we went there for a little over a year to live on my grandparents' farm, and for somebody who was used to the big city, it was like landing on the moon. But it was a great experience because I got to see how different things were in a rural setting. The lifestyle and people there were unlike anything I'd seen before. Even at that early age, it helped me become fascinated with how different people are and what it is that makes them who they are—which naturally led to my work in behavioral profiling.

But that would come later. First, I went to college at California State University, Long Beach to study criminal justice, and then the University of La Verne for public administration. I began what would become a 22-year career in the Federal Bureau of Investigation (FBI) in 1985 when I applied through the Los Angeles Field Office. By then I was a police officer with the Chino Police Department focusing on juvenile matters. When I applied to the Bureau, I underwent a variety of tests, including one called "the red handle" where the firing pin is removed from a gun so they could assess how many times I could pull the trigger without it. It seemed silly, but if I didn't have the finger strength, it would definitely impact how well I shot a weapon once I got to Quantico.

They couldn't make it convenient and have all of the tests done in one day. I had to keep coming back, but I came to look at that as divine intervention since each time I came back, so did a man named Dale. A helicopter pilot in the U.S. Marine Corp, he applied in Los Angeles for the FBI at the same time I did. For each one of those tests we happened to be at the field office at the same time. I didn't remember Dale that well, but I must've made an impression on him since he later told me he knew I was someday going to marry him. We ended up spending four and a half months in the same FBI academy class at Quantico, and that was where and when we began to develop a relationship. By the time I received orders for my first office in Albuquerque, New Mexico, Dale had indeed asked me to marry him, but his orders were for across the country in Tampa, Florida. Since both of us had been married before, we thought it would be wise to take our relationship beyond the artificial environment of Quantico to see how it worked in the real world. Dale flew out to see me every other weekend. We got married about a year later, and I was transferred to the Tampa office.

With that, Dale and I became one of the first married agent couples assigned to the same FBI office, and they didn't quite know what to do with us. The Tampa office wasn't that small. Dale was on the drug and organized crime squad working mafia-type things, and I was on the violent crimes squad. As a result, we weren't even working on the same floor. Still, the special agent in charge called us both in on our first day and said that we were not allowed to fraternize. More specifically, we were not even allowed to be seen together or to talk to each other. We were both professional people with prior careers, and we were in our thirties. Dale later asked me, "Do they think we are going to play grab-by-grabby behind closed files?" I thought, *Here I am on my squad with nine other men. I can go out to lunch or dinner with them, but I'm not allowed to be seen with my own husband.* It was ridiculous, but we respectfully said, "Yes, sir!" We complied—and we carried it off so well that I think people forgot we were married at all. Eventually, though, Dale was transferred to the same squad as me, and we remained in the same division for six months until he was relocated to a different area. That was a good thing since our working styles were so different that it created some issues at home. I am a recovering workaholic who thought nothing of taking work home. He has always been better at balance. After the transfer, our young marriage continued to thrive, as did our respective careers.

At the FBI, I first worked as a field investigator doing a myriad of investigations on predominately criminal cases like fugitives, bank robberies, and kidnapping. I then became a supervisor in San Diego, California covering white collar offenses such as public corruption and financial institution fraud. From there, I became the assistant special agent in charge for Colorado and Wyoming working out of Denver before being appointed special agent in charge of Los

Angeles. There I had counterintelligence, counterterrorism, and cybersecurity under my jurisdiction, in addition to the SWAT team and the rapid deployment teams that go over to places such as Afghanistan to serve as force protection for the military as well as doing investigative work.

Then, shortly after the terrorist attacks of 9/11, I was asked to return to FBI headquarters to work in the FBI's cybersecurity division, where I was the first female assistant director of the FBI Cyber Division. I stayed there for several years before being allowed to go back into the field as an investigator in Phoenix, Arizona so that Dale and I could move my mother from California and help take care of her as she dealt with cancer. In all, I became one of only a few women to serve in executive leadership in the FBI.

One highlight of my FBI career was my work in Tampa as coordinator for the National Center for the Analysis of Violent Crime assisting criminal profilers in Quantico. If there was any case in the Tampa/St. Petersburg area that police or sheriff investigators needed help solving, it was my job to work with them and obtain certain evidence criteria to take to Quantico because homicide is not a federal violation and the FBI doesn't have jurisdiction. That was how I became familiar with what our profilers did—and many years later I became the first female profiler in the FBI's Behavioral Analysis Unit, the same unit portrayed in the TV show "Criminal Minds." I didn't have any direct input into the show, but Jim Clemente, a former profiler who came into the unit about a year after I left, wrote for the show and became one of their main consultants. As Jim and I got to know one another, I eventually consulted on other TV shows and learned that they can either accept or reject your advice. I could say, "That would never happen that way," and they can counter, "Yeah, but we like it anyway." For what it's worth, a lot of the storylines on "Criminal Minds" are quite accurate because they are based on real cases. What isn't accurate, though, is the technology used, the time frames portrayed, and some of the relationship dynamics. For the longest time, I was not a fun person with whom to watch TV or see a movie. I'd always say, "Oh, that would never happen." I forgot how to be a kid and have fun, but I have since changed that. I can now overlook inaccuracies and get with the storylines and characters.

A profiler's duties depend on what they are being asked to do. When I was with the unit, we worked several cases involving serial killers. With those, we looked at the victimology of the women involved, since 99 percent of the victims were women. We tried to ascertain what the victims or crime scenes had in common. Other times postmortem issues regarding how the person died told a story. Link analysis, examining if all the killings were the same type of crimes, could also reveal answers, as did offender traits and characteristics. What is the offender like? What type of a person are we looking for? A variety of factors played into the profiles we created.

One of the more interesting opportunities I had during my time as a profiler was advising actress Jodie Foster in her role as Clarice Starling in the movie "Silence of the Lambs." I was very impressed with her professionalism. She took the role very seriously and came prepared with what I thought were great questions such as, "Would an agent actually respond this way?" or, "Being the only female here, would you be more stoic, or are you trying to be one of the guys?"

I told Foster that you never want to be one of the guys, but you do need to fit into the culture to be taken seriously. I see now in retrospect how that attitude influenced a lot of my actions, since I didn't respond to things the way I normally would've because I was practicing learned behavior. Today, I feel more freedom to lighten up and do things that I would never have done in the FBI because of knowing I needed to be taken seriously. Another thing Foster did was what we called the "yellow brick road," a Marine Corps obstacle course featured at the beginning of the movie. She was initially going to have her double do that part, but I asked her, "Why not do it yourself?" She was in good shape. She was a little younger than me. She worked with the physical training unit and was able to do the obstacle course herself.

My two-plus decades in the FBI benefited me because I had the privilege of working and associating with some of the most intelligent, ethical, and accomplished people I've ever known. My service in the FBI also afforded me new and different opportunities that were the most rewarding experiences in my life. Being an agent also fulfilled my two callings: serving a nation of laws and liberties and protecting others from bullies.

———

After my tenure at the FBI ended in 2006, I entered the corporate world in 2007, first at the Phoenix-area office for KPMG, a multinational professional services network where I spent 18 months helping them launch an investigative practice to protect the clients using their financial audit, tax, and advisory offerings. It was a great learning experience, but when Dale received an opportunity to serve as a SWAT commander in Los Angeles, we moved back to the west coast, and I went to work for the Southern California Edison Company (SCE). I served as the chief security officer charged with transforming security services for SCE's national infrastructure. I was primarily responsible for business resiliency, including the creation and management of SCE's emergency operations center, threat management program, information asset security, and intelligence and risk analysis. I oversaw compliance, investigations, and executive protection, and assumed a leadership role in developing external partnerships with federal, state, and local law enforcement. I also forged public/private alliances with security entities. It was engaging work, and it allowed an equally significant transition to happen in my life and marriage. The changes I experienced then—my mom passing away, Dale and I not working together for the first time, and my decision to be baptized—served as catalysts into an almost new identity. Giving my life to God also gave me a greater sense of internal serenity, purpose, gratitude, and compassion. The combination of the renewal of those positive forces brought tremendous joy to my life.

I remained at SCE for six years before transitioning in 2014 to my current employer, Herbalife. Today, I serve there as vice president of global security. I am responsible for all security functions throughout the company including executive protection, physical security, event security, employee and property security, and investigations, as well as business continuity and incident response. I also lead as chair of Herbalife's Cybersecurity Steering Team. A multi-level marketing business model equipping entrepreneurs in 94 countries, Herbalife actually had no formal security operations when I arrived, so I built all the fundamentals. Now I travel extensively building a team of regional security advisors for the company who report directly to my corporate team of 15 individuals.

One of the interesting and sad things I've noticed in the corporate security arena is that there are fewer women in that industry than there are in law enforcement. If I had the time and opportunity, I'd love to conduct research to find out if that's the case because women are simply not attracted to this field, or if it's because they are not being promoted or treated well within the industry. Gratefully, I had the chance to serve this summer on a panel discussing those very issues, and I hope to take what I learned to help bring more women into corporate security. The panel discussion, along with the ensuing audience conversation, seemed to indicate a combination of lack of interest and knowledge about the corporate security field. In addition, there was an absence or infrequency of promotional opportunities for women once they were in the security field. It is my hope these trends will change in the future.

———

As a female leader, I believe leadership can be taught, but I also think leadership can be in your DNA and can be enhanced with education. In my opinion, nothing is a substitute for experience. My definition of leadership comes from President Dwight D. Eisenhower, who said leadership "is the art of getting someone else to do something you want done because he wants to do it." If someone thinks it is their idea, or if you are able to align them with a goal or vision of where you need to go, then everybody pursues it as a team. I love teamwork. A rewarding example was when several of our regional senior vice presidents requested a security advisor in their regions to be supported by their budgets. They asked me to execute a measure that is a fundamental security component because they saw the need and appreciated the teamwork that would result.

The common thread is how you deal with people and conduct your relationship with them. I try to begin with a level playing field and give people the benefit of the doubt. I have been able to leverage that to cultivate and maintain positive professional relationships. As a leader, you should be genuine, be respectful, and always follow your values. Being honest and acting with integrity have never served me in a negative fashion. Ethics mean a great deal to me as well. I won't work for an organization or in a position where ethics aren't respected. These are the things that have kept me grounded and helped me in every position I've had in my career.

Of course, my faith is the center of my life. Christianity is what truly grounds me, and I can't give it enough credit. My mom attended one year of school to become a Presbyterian minister before she got married. My dad was an atheist. Yet when I was a child, she would sneak me into church when he went to work. We read the Bible and the Lord's Prayer. I wasn't baptized because my dad wouldn't allow it, but I insisted on it when I was an adult. Dale and I attend church as faithfully as possible. If I am not on a plane on a Sunday, I go to church wherever I am. I enjoy the diversity and fellowship that comes with being with other believers in

Christ. The community experiences I've had at church have specifically helped me with service and proven to be quite fulfilling. It has been rewarding serving meals at homeless shelters in Los Angeles and assisting at The Door of Hope and other community service organizations.

I can't really point to a particular biblical teaching or verse that informs my servant leadership style and execution. Rather, it's everything Scripture teaches in its totality that is humbling and influences me to be a servant leader. I look ahead to what is still in store for my life and my career.

Jana Monroe plans to serve God by continuing to give back and help others, staying connected and engaged with her church and community, and hopes to do more public speaking to share ideas, knowledge, and experiences designed to motivate and encourage others. Contact Jana at Janamo@herbalife.com.

6

The Journey of Faith in the Impossible

Sharon Wamble-King

IN MY CHURCH, and around South Berkeley, California where I was born, I was known as the miracle baby. People assumed and believed that God had a special destiny for me.

I don't recall that presumption being shared with me directly. I just know that I was always expected to be excellent. I don't remember anything else.

My parents moved from Arkansas to California during World War II to work in the Bay Area shipping yards. My mother, Thula, and father, Dorn, really wanted children, but my mother was diagnosed as being clinically sterile. Yet any time she went to church, she stood up and asked for prayer to have a baby. For ten years she did that in every service she attended—and her faith in the impossible reminded congregants of the biblical stories of women like Sarah, Hannah, and Elizabeth who were barren but prayed to have children who were predestined for divine excellence.

One day, an evangelist named Bishop Paige came to my mother's church. He said, "Anyone here who wants to have a baby, get in line. I want to pray for you. When you get pregnant, you will have multiple children. I have testimonies in my wallet I can show you." To my knowledge, my mother never saw one of those testimonies, but she did get in line—and, sure enough, she became pregnant. When she went to the doctor's office, they were stunned. They heard two heartbeats when they examined her, but because of her prior diagnosis and her older age, they thought the heartbeats were a sign she was going to have a severely deformed child. It was too abnormal.

She was defiant. "God did this," she declared, "and I'm going to have the baby."

It wasn't until she went into labor that they discovered there actually *were* two heartbeats. She was going to have twins. Multiple babies, just like Bishop Paige had prophesied.

Sadly, my brother did not survive. The umbilical cord was wrapped around his neck, and he had respiratory distress. I was tiny at just over three pounds, and I ended up staying in intensive care for months. The expectation then was that I wasn't going to live for long, but the community of faith in Berkeley went to work praying for me to live because they all knew about the story of my mother's pregnancy.

When I finally came home from the hospital, everyone referred to me as the miracle baby. Many years later, while

I was working as a business management consultant with William M. Mercer in San Francisco, I conducted a focus group of Medicare recipients. A woman came up to me and said, "You are Thula's baby, aren't you?"

I smiled. "Yeah."

She turned to everyone else in the room. "Lawd, let me tell you all about this miracle baby." She shared the entire story about my mother's faith—and of God doing the impossible.

So, the miracle baby legacy, and the presumption of divine destiny that went with it, stayed with me all through my years in the Bay Area. But instead of letting it put pressure on me, I have accepted that predestination to excellence, allowing it be the foundation and inspiration for everything I did as a young person, all that I do today, and all that I teach others about being a woman in leadership.

My journey of faith in the impossible was just getting started.

———

When I was only five, my father said the principal at my school approached him, wanting me to give a special speech for the Christmas program. It was a full page in length, but everyone knew I could do it. That's just the way it was when I was a kid. I always got straight A's. If I came home with a B, my father said there was room for improvement. I can understand his motivation for me to do my very best. He didn't finish eighth grade because he had to leave school to take care of his family. That was the narrative of the times for him and other blacks born and raised in the Jim Crow south—doing your best to be a credit to your race.

During a trip to Arkansas to visit family when I was four, my aunt, who taught at an all-black school, dressed me up to show me off to her fifth-grade class. I recall how slowly everyone spoke when they responded to her and being amazed at how the students struggled to answer her questions as I sat in the back of the classroom that day. "You don't know *that?*" I proclaimed time and again. My aunt eventually had to tell me to be quiet.

Later, at recess, she took me down to see my uncle, the principal, in his office, where the superintendent of schools, a white man, was visiting. Everyone else was at attention and on their best behavior for his visit. Not knowing any better, I ran right over and jumped into his lap. "Hi, how are you doing? What's your name? Do you have any kids? What are their names?" Frozen in place, my aunt couldn't breathe. Everybody in the hall couldn't believe it. I was just chitchatting with him, and he started talking to me. We had a little conversation, a little black girl on a white man's lap, in 1950's Arkansas.

I was precocious and conversational, mainly because I was the only child in a home filled with adults, and those were traits that certainly helped me fit in as I grew up in the radical Bay Area of the 1960's. Berkeley was segregated then, and my father was a staunch civil rights activist. So was my mother and the whole family. As a kid, I took part in civil rights marches and demonstrations for fair housing and equal rights. My parents were big believers in integrated schools because their experiences in the south showed how segregated schools did not provide the quality of education they should've. Therefore, they sacrificed, moving to a different neighborhood so my brother and I could have an opportunity to go to an integrated school. I finally did just that for the first time in sixth grade, and I made the honor roll. The next year, though, I had to return to a segregated school while my father and many other parents led a fight to allow black students to attend the all-white school in the El Cerrito hills. They prevailed, and I was among the first 100 black kids from the segregated school to go to the all-white one.

I'll never forget the first day of eighth grade. I entered the classroom and immediately thought there was something very different about my fellow students—and it had nothing to do with skin color. The teacher came over to me.

"Spell cat," she directed.

I thought she was crazy. "C-A-T."

She handed me a lollipop.

Whoa! This is what school is like here? You get a lollipop for spelling cat?

I told my father, and he discovered I had been placed in the mentally handicapped class. Despite my honor achievements at the segregated school and strong academics in earlier grades, I had taken an IQ test years earlier in elementary school and, unbeknownst to my parents, had scored very low. I was one of those people who struggle when taking standardized tests. Apparently, that IQ score was used as an excuse to place me in a classroom with the mentally handicapped kids. The mistake was fixed, and I continued to excel. In fact, by the next quarter, I was placed in gifted classes and was the only black person in most of them. I was even named student of the month for the entire school.

In high school, I joined with about 25 black students from the original 100, and we worked with our parents to lobby the school's counselor to allow us to become tutors to students who were in junior high school. We wanted them to learn the lessons we had so that they could persevere and succeed in high school. The counselor championed our efforts, and we saw ourselves as being these cool, teen rebels, a part of the whole fabric of activism during a tumultuous time of racial protest in the Bay Area. We believed the only way we had the credibility to be heard and to do these radical things was to be excellent, and we were. We got really good grades. We did extracurricular activities. I was in the marching band and the orchestra. All of us were in all kinds of things. Our group made sure there was a black person in everything, determined to achieve equal opportunity. There was a black person in the German club and the Russian club. We made sure that the teachers taught black history. We banded together, feeling we were going to change the world. I suppose we did, at least in our little corner of it. In spite of all the opposition (racial slurs were commonplace when we were discussed in school board meetings) we still achieved high GPA's. All 25 of us ended up going to college. Most of us went to graduate school, and many earned post-graduate professional degrees. It was evidence of how we were predestined for excellence and ended up achieving what others would've never thought possible.

Of course, my journey to faith in the impossible was nurtured as I accepted Jesus Christ as my Savior at age seven and attended Church of God in Christ churches throughout my upbringing. So, as I first entered college on an academic scholarship at the University of the Pacific, the morals of my faith naturally informed my actions. I wanted a boyfriend, but because I was a Christian, I wasn't participating in pre-marital sex, and I wasn't going to play the game to have one. While I didn't have a boyfriend, my love of contemporary gospel music was evident as I played everything from Tramaine Hawkins to Andraé Crouch in my dorm room. One of the fellow students who sometimes stopped by to see me was a dee-jay for the campus radio station and the most popular black guy at the school. He asked if he could borrow some of my records to play on his radio show. I let him, and the phones lit up with people liking what they heard.

When he came back to borrow more, he challenged, "I dare you to go to the radio station and get your own show." I thought, *This is a private university of 5,000 with about 100 black people and a bunch of rich, white folks. Why not?* But I figured there was no way I could do it because I had never even been inside a radio station. Nevertheless, I grabbed a cassette player and recorded my own show, then asked for an appointment with the station manager, Irwin. I believed that if the Lord allowed me to get in front of him, present my argument for my own show, and he said "yes," then God was going to be my copartner in it. Irwin had a big, red handlebar mustache and was known for being gruff. "I hope this isn't a waste of my time," he commented. I boldly pitched my show, and that was all I needed. He didn't even listen to the cassette. "Would you like one hour or two?"

Not only did I host the show, I ended up getting a license so that I could engineer it myself. I knew nothing about broadcasting or communications, but I excelled. That began a process that led to me going to graduate school at San Diego State University, and that led to a journalism internship at the area CBS-affiliated television station as a story writer and reporter when, again, I had never previously written a news story in my life. I just believed that if I was put in a position to do something, it was for a reason and God would help me get it done. My faith in the impossible was growing. That station later ended up giving me a scholarship for graduate school.

———

As I entered the workforce, each opportunity allowed me to achieve more seemingly impossible things, all while learning new principles about leadership. I worked a variety of different jobs after graduate school before landing at Kaiser Permanente, the integrated managed care health system based in Oakland, California, in 1986, which was where I worked for the next eight-and-a-half years in roles including public affairs before I served on their executive staff.

At Kaiser Permanente, I discovered that I am a values-driven individual. Health care resonated with me because it was service oriented. It helped people. It had direct impact on the lives of millions to not only improve individuals, but their families and communities as well. That spoke directly to who I was as a professional and as a Christian. The values of service, integrity, caring, nurturing, and communicating to people with empathy were so important, and I was the custodian of those organizational values and integrity to our patients, members, families, and the community as a whole. It was wonderful to have an impactful, high-quality, enlightening and enhancing experience in their lives.

The fact that I'm values driven also reminds me that all of us have been put on this planet by God at this particular time for a very specific role. We are on divine assignment—and learning early on what makes your heart sing will give you the courage to go through all the ups and downs to pursue your destiny in Him and achieve the impossible in your life.

My time at Kaiser Permanente was followed by over two years of service at William M. Mercer as a consultant. I was first introduced to the concepts of change management at Kaiser, but at Mercer I began to learn the concepts of management consulting. It was another instance where I didn't have a clue going in, but I was able to be bold, move forward, and learn. I found out that a consultant is not just someone who provides strategic counsel. A consultant also has to prospect, identify potential clients, and sell. It was a whole new skill set, and I thought I knew how to do it because I had been an internal consultant at Kaiser, but what I learned at Mercer was completely different. In addition, I had to become competent in consulting in the midst of tremendous adversity because there was a lot of push back for me being there in the first place. I did not come through the normal ranks as a consultant. Many people start straight from college, but I came from the corporate arena. Therefore, I had to pull myself together and understand how to seek out the right advice and from whom to get it.

I spent hours reading about consulting, and there were times when I felt like I was sinking in quicksand, but I never believed I had failed. I always trusted that God had put me there for a reason. I needed to learn what it took not just to survive, but to succeed and thrive. I became convinced that thriving was much more of a reflection of God's nature and an opportunity for me to show who He was in those situations. I found that I could show the fruits of His Spirit as I climbed uphill, learned a whole new way of thinking and of being, and took on a whole new identity as a consultant.

When we are faced with difficulties, challenges, and the seemingly impossible, where does our vision come from? Where does our courage and strength originate? What is our purpose? At Mercer, my purpose was to reflect God's nature in the way that He would behave and lead in that situation. I was the only African American in my office. Many times, I was the only African American consultant on the team. I had to deal with preconceived notions that I was in my position as a consultant because of affirmative action. I confronted power and status in a way that I hadn't before. What keeps us standing up and our eyes focused on God in those moments? What keeps the elasticity in our resilience? It comes from knowing that we have purpose and by becoming adaptable and irrepressible in the face of our challenges. Interestingly, I went to Bible college while I was at Mercer. Being there became a catalyst to excel further spiritually. Often, it is in our greatest difficulties where we find opportunity to grow closer to God and know Him in a deeper way.

Next, I received an opportunity to work with Arthur Andersen, LLP, also in San Francisco, where I directed large-scale change engagements for a variety of Fortune 500 clients. Arthur Anderson was a tough environment where the utmost excellence and expertise were expected. Again, I was one of two African Americans in the practice, and there were not very many women in management ranks, either. All of the challenges of being a person of color and a woman in a very male environment, and of being a Christian where values of integrity and ethics came into play, were constants at Arthur Anderson. Several times, I was placed in a situation where a client or partner wanted me to do something that created the ethical dilemma of how to respond appropriately. I learned that many people in the firm built relationships with people at the top because they wanted to be promoted. It was all about getting ahead.

I relied on the counsel of Romans 12:1-2, that tells us, "in view of God's mercy, to offer your bodies as a living sacrifice, holy and pleasing to God—this is your true and proper worship. Do not conform to the pattern of this world, but be transformed by the renewing of your mind. Then you will be able to test and approve what God's will is—his good, pleasing and perfect will." As I did this, I began to stand out, not only because of the excellence I brought to my work, but because of my behavior, ethics, values, and what I *didn't* do. I saw myself as the distinct jewel in the midst of other jewels. I had to be positive. I had to learn executive presence. I discovered how to fearlessly and uniquely interact with CEO's and CFO's and directors of the board because of who I was in God.

We need to be confident and have the courage that comes from an understanding that we are here for a reason and have been chosen for this place and for this time in history to do what may seem impossible. Build the right kind of relationships based upon the right criteria. Have a perspective driven by your mission. Don't be like other leaders where you're at the top and everyone else are minions who follow after you because they are in your downstream. Instead, look at Jesus with His disciples. He didn't look down on them. They were a part of His team. If you lead the way Jesus did—incorporating people, having dialogue with them, and challenging them while nurturing and loving them—you will be distinct. In the corporate world, this may not always be seen as the best thing to do, but it is the right thing to do. It is the *righteous* thing to do.

————

After that, I took all that I had developed professionally up to that point and launched my own company, The Wambleking Group, in Castro Valley, California. It was designed to provide clients with advice and counsel for strategic communication and change management services, and my roles included government and community relations work. During this time, I discovered that having your own business is hard. People glamorize it by focusing on how you can be your own boss, control things for yourself, and make your own hours, and all of that is true. But you are everything from the CEO to the custodian. You must learn how to do payroll, keep employees, and manage other people who don't report to you. It becomes a 24-7 sort of existence to build and expand your business. Therefore, you must acquire the flexibility, agility, mindset, and, above all, the perseverance to succeed. I had to learn how to approach clients and ensure their financial success as well as mine. It was different in so many ways than what I'd experienced previously in corporate settings. The responsibility and accountability rests with you—your vision, your mission, your values, and your execution. You have to be tenacious and resilient.

Sometimes I was selling my services by myself; other times, I was doing it with a member of my team. In either case, I found that selling is more about the relationships that are formed than it is about the services you offer. People buy *you* and your ability to connect with them so that they know that you are their partner for success professionally and personally. I learned to ask questions like, "How do I resonate with those clients who have issues and want a solution?" "How do I ask the right questions and not make assumptions?" I discovered that if I add value and build the kind of relationships that are sustainable, the money will follow.

I returned to the traditional workforce after my professional colleagues shared with me an opportunity that they thought would be great for me where I could leverage my experience as a consultant and a strategist. It started with Aetna, Inc. in Hartford, Connecticut for nearly two years as vice president for communication strategy and internal communication. Then I moved on to a large health insurer based in Florida where I spent almost nine years overseeing communications to ensure stakeholder alignment and engagement in the organization's strategic direction.

At those companies, my leadership abilities and knowledge grew as I realized that people in all levels of an organization have value. It is a tapestry, and we are all intertwined. Sadly, employees who are in lower level positions are often hesitant to interact with executives because of the company's history or cultural norms. But I strived to be someone who could be approached formally or informally as a mentor. After all, people were watching everything I did, and I was beginning to understand that I was leading and influencing others even when I didn't realize it. One time I spoke at work about my journey. Afterward, a young lady came up to me and said, "You really made me feel so proud to be an African

American woman." Then she began to talk about herself in a very negative way, focusing on the fact that she didn't have a college degree.

"Wait a minute," I told her. "Let's go talk." When I invited her to my office in the executive suite, she insisted, "I'm not allowed to go up there."

I took her hand, pulled her into the elevator, and took her up to the executive floor. She nervously said, "Oh, if my boss' boss sees me up here, I'm gonna get in trouble."

"If you get in trouble, call me," I said as I led her into my office. I closed the door, cancelled my next appointments, and ended up talking to her for about an hour. I started with her self-esteem and her view of herself because of her lack of a degree. I spoke to her about the God-given rights she had and that she was at the company for a reason. I concluded, "Love all of the things you have done well and look at yourself differently."

About a year later, she told me, "After talking to you, I went and applied for a job that I never thought I would be qualified for. I was scared, but I got the position. You changed my life forever." Today, she has adopted me as family.

You just can't get that kind of influence from reading a book or taking a training class on leadership. You get it from leading with your heart. I had empathy that the young woman could be so much more than she could ever believe herself to be. That is what leadership is. It's not a title or position. I think to myself, *If I am excellent at what I am doing, and if I anticipate the future, innovate, and really think strategically about the unique value I can bring to someone, I will get the next opportunity and be ready for it.* Focus on growing, learning, and doing your best, and the opportunities will come to your door, likely in a different way than you thought. Always be ready—because there is a divine architect. One of my mentors describes God as the grand overarching designer. He stands before you, beside you, and behind you. He'll help you have the courage and the confidence to be all that you can be.

In June 2014, I relaunched The Wambleking Group in Jacksonville, Florida. I focused on strategic communication, stakeholder engagement and advocacy, change management, and leadership development. As I returned to being self-employed, I also looked for ways to learn and to grow. I worked with a coach because I saw the relaunch as an opportunity for me to step back from the career I had and do what Scripture tells me to do in Romans 12: renew my mind. It's hard to renew our minds when we are working an 18-hour day. This became a divine sabbatical from corporate work, given to me by God, that also created opportunities to work with other incredible people. One of the ways I did that was by joining the John Maxwell Team, being certified as a teacher, speaker and coach. Through it, I met people who are now a part of my family that I would never have encountered had I continued my career the way it was going. I started a PhD program in leadership and change. I learned about the connection of neuroscience to leadership. I was able to do things I had imagined but never really thought I could do—and my journey of faith in the impossible progressed to an entirely new level.

In this transition, I discovered the importance of self-care. While I was an executive, I ran myself ragged. I know

now that my personal and spiritual development is as important, if not more so, as my leadership development. If I don't take care of the temple (body) that God gave me, I can't do what He wants me to do. Find whatever it is that is healing to your soul—meditation, prayer, relaxation, praise and worship music—and make time for it so that you can heal from being bitter or rejected and from all of the other things that people did that were so damaging to your psyche and that you don't understand. You have to heal from those things before you can go to the next level because the next level requires you to be a different person.

Today, I continue to lead The Wambleking Group while serving a new role as leader of the corporate communications division at Geisinger Health, which includes internal communication, executive communications, media relations, and issues management for health systems of 32,000 employees, including 11 hospitals, and more than 250 clinic sites. I suppose anyone looking at my resume would be impressed—but I see it all as simply a realization of the expectation of excellence that is my legacy, and the ongoing fulfillment of the destiny God has graciously provided for me.

I am inspired by the book, *Jesus, CEO: Using Ancient Wisdom for Visionary Leadership*, by Laurie Beth Jones. In it, she tells how Christ took 12 diverse individuals and became their leader before He left them. Then they went and changed the world. They did the impossible with somebody who was the impossible. Born of a virgin, simultaneously both God and man, Jesus was the very embodiment of the impossible. The journey of the impossible is just that: a journey. We have to go on that journey to have our lives positioned in faith.

It has been through my journey that I am learning to trust in God as *my* leader. I have learned how to lead by looking at Him. Through God, I know what it means to care about the people I influence—even when they aren't saying what I want them to say or doing what I want them to do—and to be patient, kind, and love them like He does. Now, when I face a leadership challenge, the first thing I think is, *God, give me the ability to see this situation the way that it really is. Give me the ability to behave, say, think, and feel the way you would because you are the ultimate leader.* If I can trust in Him as my leader, I know that I will continually change and evolve as the leader He wants me to be. That way, those I lead can add value, reach their potential, and have the best life possible to achieve the impossible.

As a doctoral student in leadership and change at Antioch University, I recently wrote an essay on reflective leadership. In it, I concluded that no matter how successful I am professionally, I am hollow without a balanced focus on my own personal and professional development. I am more self-aware today than at any time in my life, and I am open to emerging opportunities to serve authentically and make a difference. With God's help, I have learned valuable lessons, and I can realistically express pride and gratitude for achieving results with people while remaining true to the values and virtues instilled within me decades ago. I have maintained wholeness and a commitment to faith and excellence in all aspects of my life: family, church, community, and work.

Not bad for a miracle baby, wouldn't you say?

Sharon Wamble-King is president of The WambleKing Group, LLC and passionate communicator who possesses decades of experience in corporate, consulting, ecumenical, and not-for-profit environments. She helps people and organizations transform to leverage market opportunities, mitigate risks, and achieve visionary goals as an accomplished change leadership/communication strategist. Contact Sharon at swambleking@thewamblekinggroup.com.

7

A Life Worth Living

Amarie Whetten

IN A WAY, it's natural that I'm devoted to helping women find health and joy when I consider how often I've had to deal with death—especially knowing the amazing God who has helped me find my own personal wellness and happiness through His consistent love and healing touch.

After earning my chemical engineering degree from the University of Colorado-Boulder in 1996 and completing grad school four years later, I have worked for 22 years in the corporate world, first at Hewlett-Packard and later at Raytheon, during which time I met and married my husband, Chris. I now have four children, Kate, Leah, Sophie, and Kyle, and in the summer of 2019 we moved from Tucson, Arizona to Huntsville, Alabama so I could carry on as an engineer while developing my own business as a Juice Plus+ representative, an organization I first discovered after I began dealing with severe auto immunity issues. As a representative for Juice Plus+, I not only tell people about the company's products, but I also help them grow their own business.

Just a few years ago, I was in so much pain and discomfort that I'd have to hold my sides and squeeze in on my abdomen when I stood up to talk with anyone. As I started working with a life coach and a naturopath, I learned I had developed over 50 different food allergies to things as normal as green beans or black pepper. To boost my auto immune system, I did a cleanse diet for 90 days and then started juicing with a focus on fruits and vegetables. Although I was feeling better, the very process of using the juicer felt like a part-time job because there was so much cleaning and upkeep involved. That's when I met a woman at church who told me about Juice Plus+. I was excited to learn how the company had concentrated the product into a capsule, which was much easier to use than juicing. I felt better right away with the help of their capsules, and after a little more research, I decided I wanted to help others discover what Juice Plus+ could do for them. I began by hosting in-home events to talk to people about wellness and exercise, self-care, rest, and nutrition—and now I get to travel all over the country representing the company. I focus on female clients, and I've helped them get off of their pharmaceutical medications. Even two Type 2 diabetics have gone into remission, and my parents have gotten off of blood pressure medication.

The exciting results inspire me, yet I wouldn't be where I am—or who I am—had it not been for the experiences and lessons learned from my past.

Born in Estes Park, Colorado in 1974, my mother Julia was a homemaker while my father, Harv, was a human resources director with government social services. Both were entrepreneurial with side businesses going on: my father was a realtor and a car salesman who also sold cords of wood, and my mother had a beauty business in which clients saw her at home. I had three siblings. My older brother, Mike, was adopted from South Korea after my parents got married and could not conceive. They successfully navigated the international adoption process, and when they found out they were getting my brother, my mom realized she was pregnant with me. My brother and I are about 14 months apart in age. My younger brother, Steve, came along four years later, and then four years after he was born, my sister Annelise completed the family.

I spent my days falling in love with the lush, rustic nature that surrounded Estes Park, riding bikes, hiking, and jumping on trampolines. Dad was super fun-loving. He'd get home from work and take us fishing, so mom could fry up freshly-caught trout for dinner. In school, I developed an affinity for math and science, but it was my high school chemistry teacher who introduced me to engineering. She encouraged me to go to an engineering camp during the summer heading into my senior year of high school. That lit a fire under me and helped lead to my decision to pursue chemical engineering in college.

My early childhood, really, was nothing short of ideal. My parents were good Baptists who followed all the rules, so they had a role model-type relationship with me that was loving and fun. At times, my mom would get angry at my dad, but he never pushed back. He avoided confrontation.

Yet it was when my grandfather passed away when I was in fourth grade that things started to change. His death had a significant impact on my dad. His father was his foundation from financial decision-making to his perspective on other choices of right and wrong. That death began to slowly alter the path of our family as my dad gradually lost his bearings. Things became strained between my parents over time. After a while, dad didn't know what to do with himself. He seemed lost.

But there was no way we could've anticipated how bad it would end up.

———

In mid-April 1991, when I was 16, my dad came under investigation for embezzlement at work. He told me about it briefly on a Wednesday morning while I was ironing a skirt before school. I asked him if he was worried. "Guess I don't need to worry," he responded, "if I haven't done anything wrong." So, I didn't think much of it again until after school that same day when I called my mom to let her know I was going to be late for dinner after a Spanish club meeting went long. When she thanked me for letting her know I was going to be tardy, I could tell from her voice that she wasn't her normal self.

I asked, "How did things go today with dad's investigation?"
She was surprised. "How did you know about that?"
I told her what little dad had told me that morning, and she revealed that he had told me about the situation even before he had discussed it with her. She then told me dad

had hired a lawyer and conceded, "I think we have something to worry about. It looks like we are in for a long, tough ride."

Things were particularly tense when I got home. The entire family talked that evening at dinner about what was happening and what it could mean: arrest, job loss, articles in the local paper, even moving to a new city. After dinner, dad sat at the dining room table alone while mom, Annelise, and I were nearby in the kitchen. Mike and Steve were elsewhere doing their homework. Annelise asked mom to tuck her into bed, and as they left, I wanted to go with them, but I knew if I did, dad might feel rejected. I didn't want that. I tried to look busy stacking dishes, and dad looked up toward me once, as though he wanted to say something, but he remained silent. Realizing he wasn't going to initiate a conversation, I offered, "It's going to be okay somehow." I then walked over to where he was sitting and gave him a hug.

His reply still rings in my ears today. "Sorry that I haven't been a good father to you."

It was awkward. I'd never seen him that way before. And I had never thought he had been a bad father.

"It's fine, dad. We will be fine. We'll get through this together as a family. I still love you. You're the best father ever."

It looked like he might start crying, but he pulled himself together, and I quickly made an excuse to leave the kitchen. I couldn't figure out why he said what he did, but much later, I thought it might have been because he didn't know what to do with me as a teenager. I was a bit of a rebel, unafraid, adventurous, and headstrong. I knew how my parents felt about things, but I largely ignored them. I thought they were sheltered and missing out. I was planning to experience the world, and it likely worried him. He took me and my friends to youth group at church every week and felt he was like a shepherd to them. Maybe he felt I was going to lead them astray. To this day, I don't know for sure.

I didn't sleep well that night.

The next day, Thursday, everything hit me during math class. My friend Sammi noticed my eyes were puffy and asked me what was wrong. I collapsed into tears as I told her what was going on. I even said it would all be in the newspapers soon, but not to tell anyone. That evening, a police officer was at our house picking up my dad's files when another friend of mine stopped by to get some hot rollers to prepare for prom the following week. I told her the officer was just a friend of my father's. Then, later that night, mom's father came by and collected all of our hunting rifles—and I shockingly knew why. It was part of a suicide watch protocol my dad had helped create for our town through his job for the county. My mind spun. *My dad's on suicide watch? Really? Is he that worried?* I preferred to think everyone was being overdramatic.

After school on Friday, I went to a movie with a couple of friends, then called home to see if it was okay for them to come over and hang around at the house. I figured with everything going on, it would be best to check. Dad answered, said it was fine, and then, after a brief hesitation, said, "I love you."

"I love you, too," I said, then hung up.

One of my friends commented how cute it was that I told my parents I loved them on the phone, and that's when I realized how unusual it actually was for dad to say that at the end of a call. By the time we got to my house, dad was already in bed. Later, my friends left, and I turned in for the night as well. Exhausted from the stress of the past few days, I slept deeply.

Dad was always an early riser, even on a Saturday. He usually got up at 5:00 a.m. to read the newspaper, but I remembered that this particular Saturday his best friend, Kirk, was coming over to take him to breakfast. I was awakened suddenly by someone pounding on the front door of the house. Knowing mom or someone else would deal with it, I rolled over and was just dozing off when I heard someone stomping down the hallway outside my room.

"Get up!" the person yelled. It was Kirk. "All of you come out here. Everyone up!"

I wearily looked at the clock. It was 8:00 a.m. I was irritated. *What the heck is this?*

I was sitting up and trying to find a pair of sweats to put on with my nightshirt when I heard someone stop in front of my bedroom door. "Get into the kitchen!" It was Kirk again.

"Just a minute! I have to find some pants."

"In a minute, you won't care if you have pants on or not!" he countered.

Still annoyed, I came out moments later and headed for the kitchen, where I heard a bunch of voices. *What in the world is all the commotion about?*

I exited the hallway to see mom holding Annelise as though she was shielding her from a chilling wind. The look mom had on her face was one I'd never seen before. I had no idea what it meant, but it frightened me.

"What's wrong?"

I addressed the question to my mother, but she didn't

respond. It was as if she didn't even hear me, though I know she surely did. I noticed that Mike and Steve were in the room, then I looked at Kirk and across to his wife, Pat. *Why is she here?* I was so confused.

"What?" I asked louder. "What happened?"

Mom, pure irritation lacing her voice, finally answered. "Your dad stabbed himself."

I immediately envisioned dad sitting in a hospital bed, with family all around and surrounding him with love, saying to us, "Sorry, kids. I just don't know what I was thinking. Sorry I scared you." In my fantasy, dad was alive, and his suicide attempt had made him realize how precious life was and how dearly he loved us. *How come he's not in here with us if he's alive?*

"Is he alright? Is he alive? He's still alive, isn't he?"

I began to panic because no one answered me. I don't know who it was who finally said that dad "wasn't going to breathe again," but those words made me sharply aware that my dad was indeed dead.

"No!" I shouted. "No! It's not true. It *can't* be true."

I couldn't breathe. I was dizzy.

I needed to see him for myself. I asked mom, "Where is he?"

"He is in the driveway," she said, then repeated, "He stabbed himself."

Mike walked past me. He was angry. "I don't believe you!" he yelled. I turned with him and followed him to the already-open front door, but the wrought iron door beyond it was still closed. Mike pushed it open, and I was only a few strides behind.

At that instant, I heard a voice clearly telling me *not* to go. I don't know if the voice was from an adult in the kitchen, from God, or from somewhere inside of me, but it made me stop at the doorway—and there I stayed as the wrought iron door slammed shut in front of me, as if in slow motion.

I abruptly knew that I did not want the last sight of my father to be his lifeless, bleeding body. I never tried to look after that, either.

Only later would I remember that the last words my dad ever said to me were, "I love you."

It was his goodbye.

————

His suicide was nothing less than catastrophic. Annelise was only eight, and dad's death seemed to hit her the hardest at first because mom remained so upset about the suicide, all of her anger reflected off onto Annelise. Today, gratefully, Annelise is a lovely, adoring mom and the best aunt ever. Steve managed to muscle his way through it, as I did, until we became adults. He is now a terrific dad and has the same fun-loving mannerisms our father had. When I tell my kids about my dad I say, "He looked just like Uncle Steve. He acted like Uncle Steve." Steve is silly. He's a joker. He's everything dad was until everything started going wrong.

Mike, who insisted on seeing dad's body, went off the rails. Harv was his foundation, and that foundation was destroyed. He eventually left home and never returned. Mike has been in and out of the federal prison system ever since, suffering from drug and alcohol addiction.

The biggest impact on me was watching my now-widowed mom, who had primarily been a homemaker for her entire adult life, try to figure out how to make ends meet, as well as how to carry on herself. Her behavior completely changed from then on. She provided shelter, clothing, and dinner, but in every other way it was like living with a 17-year-old. In time, mom would recover and remarry, but for the remainder of the time I was home, she was shattered.

It was during that time that I decided I would never *ever* be in a position where I couldn't take care of myself and my family. In fact, that was the biggest reason why I went into engineering. I was going to do everything I could to make sure I had a stable, growing job and could sustain myself.

I was never going to struggle the way mom did after dad's suicide.

———

I self-identified as a leader early on, beginning in fifth grade when I ran for class office. I became the secretary, still a stereotypically common role for girls in the late 1980s, but after one term as secretary, I decided I wanted to be class president. I didn't want to take notes. I wanted to lead. I sat at the dinner table with both of my parents helping me as I wrote my election speeches. After that, I was always in class leadership at school, all the way through to my senior year in high school when I served as student body president.

Estes Park was a small tourist community. Everyone worked beginning at age 14. I was excited to get my first paid job at a go-kart track. When I was 15, I recall telling my high school boyfriend that my dream was to be a lawyer when I grew up (this was before my chemistry teacher directed me toward engineering), and I wanted a stay-at-home husband who would take care of the house and watch the kids while I went to work. I knew that I wanted to be relevant in the workforce while having someone else co-manage the home front.

That innate drive to be a leader was always there—but after my dad died, my attitude shifted from, "I have this skill set," to "I *must* do this." I had always been a hard worker and was excited to get things done, and that only accelerated following his death. My Christian faith, meanwhile, entered into a phase of self-discovery. I grew up in church. My dad was an elder. My mom was the organist. I was in church every Sunday and every Wednesday evening. Basically, you had to be in the hospital if you were going to miss church. Dad's faith was very strong. It was normal for him to go around the house singing "How Great Thou Art" and other hymns. Christianity was such a part of our lives.

But when dad killed himself, I had to create my own faith experience. I thought the church did a horrific job with his funeral. They didn't know how to handle it. Our pastor preached something about a waterfall, a completely non-sensical, random speech that had nothing whatsoever to do with anything going on in our lives, much less about our grief. He was just using the occasion as a chance to convert souls. By the end of the funeral, I was mad. I ditched church, and I didn't really find it again until after college because I felt betrayed by the institution. I still possessed my faith, but I couldn't figure out where to practice it because I couldn't find a place where I felt connected. I tried things like Campus Crusade, but nothing ever fit.

In the meantime, detached from church and busy at school, I got together with a young man I had first met in high school. We didn't see each other much, usually on

Wednesday night and again on Sunday, but we developed a relationship that soon deepened. We started dating at the end of my senior year in high school and got married before my senior year in college. However, it wasn't until we were married and moved in together that I realized he had a problem: drinking. In fact, I quickly discovered he had a severe alcohol addiction. He hid it the entire time we were dating, and in hindsight I missed obvious clues like sneaking cherry vodka during art class in high school. As I saw his brokenness, I tried to fix it—but nothing ever worked, and why would it? I was still broken from dad's suicide.

Perhaps, then, it was natural for two broken people to stay together as long as we did, seven years. But I came to a point, around age 26, where I determined that I wanted to have children of my own, and there was no way I wanted to start a family with him. Because of what had happened with my dad, I wanted my children to have a stable father. In the end, that was the issue that drove us apart and led to our divorce. I was excelling in my professional career at Hewlett-Packard, but my personal life was a mess, and I went from broken to shattered inside.

Whose life is this? I thought. *How did this happen?*

How did my life become this tragedy?

I knew I needed a fresh start.

Incredibly, I found it—or him—three months after my ex-husband moved out. After the divorce, I decided to return to my roots of faith, and I found a church where I did feel connected to the people and to God. It was during this time that I met Chris, the brother-in-law of a classmate from chemical engineering school. We went out on a first date and then continued every weekend after that for the next 10 months until we got married in September 2002.

I knew the moment I met Chris that we would get married and that he was the one—but that was truly confirmed the night I told him about my dad's suicide. For years I had told no one. Someone would have to ask me 27 questions just to find out my dad was deceased, and even when they did, I wouldn't say how he died. When I told Chris, he didn't know what to say at first, but when I blurted, "So you don't want to be with me now, right?" he said, "What are you talking about? That's crazy. This doesn't change anything."

I still struggled with Chris' acceptance of me all the way until the day he proposed. But he did fully accept me and always had, even when I couldn't believe it.

With Chris, I felt a powerful sense of being with that *one* to whom you are divinely connected, and together we built an amazing life and family.

But, sadly, there were still other encounters with death to come.

During the summer of 2015, I felt a prompting from God, what I call a "tap on the shoulder," to return to Colorado to visit my brother Steve, sister-in-law Kelda, and their two boys, one-year-old Elliott and his older brother, Emmett. I had developed a morning routine of prayer, journaling, and doing a daily affirmation, and had come to trust in these cues from the Lord. They meant I was either supposed to go do something, or something was supposed to happen that I needed to be a part of.

In this case, it meant a change of plans. We were originally planning a family trip to Austin, Texas, but when I told my husband about the God tap, he agreed we should heed it. I had a sense that, indeed, something significant was getting ready to take place. I didn't know why, but I posted a message on Facebook on the drive there, saying, "All we have in the moment is to love the people we are with. We should appreciate them now because we don't know how long we get to be with them."

We spent a week with my brother and his family, and all was going wonderful. Little Elliott had just had surgery a month earlier on a lung defect and seemed to be thriving. Then, right at the end of that week while Chris and I were away at his sister's house, Elliott suddenly stopped breathing. Steve, Kelda, my mom, and my stepdad, Claude, watched in horror as my sister, Annelise, tried to resuscitate him. He was rushed by Flight for Life to the children's hospital in Denver and put on life support, but he didn't survive.

Despite the pain, it was important to have been there for the last week of Elliott's life. It allowed our kids to experience the grief of losing someone, which has helped them to understand the grief that I survived with the loss of my father. In addition, it was from our grief that Chris and I decided to have another child, Kyle, which we did in 2017.

I started my business with Juice Plus+ as a representative shortly before that fateful trip to Colorado in 2015, and not long afterward I took on my friend Megan as a business partner. Megan and I had known each other since my days at Hewlett-Packard where she was my supervisor, and our relationship started growing after she threw me a wedding shower when Chris and I got married. That was when my husband met her husband, Cory. They started playing volleyball together, and we started going out with them regularly as couples. That brought us really close together. Eventually, Megan and Cory had three children, Cameron, Payton, and Addison. While we were all separated for a while after we moved to Tucson for my job at Raytheon, they eventually relocated to the desert southwest so we could raise our families together. In 2017, an employment change caused them to move to Huntsville, but we remained close and continued working Juice Plus+ together.

On the morning of December 14, 2018, Megan and I had a call scheduled. I texted her to confirm that we were still meeting with her client.

She immediately texted back, "Cameron is dead."

Shocked, I tried to call right away, but she didn't pick up. She texted a few minutes later to let me know that the FBI and emergency personnel were at her house at that moment. Suddenly I pictured Megan's 17-year-old son, who I had known since he was a toddler catching frogs, snakes, and tarantulas, lying dead.

Then I called my husband, and while he had not heard what happened, he instantly reached his own conclusion.

"Amarie, Cameron killed himself."

Dear God, I thought, and briefly flashed back to my father's suicide, then to little Elliott's death, still so fresh. "Maybe it was a car accident," I responded, verbalizing my denial of the harsh truth. Yet Chris had been worried about Cameron for a while and suspected the worst. *Lord, another death? What is happening?*

Megan confirmed that Cameron indeed committed suicide, and I got on the next flight from Tucson to Huntsville to help with the funeral arrangements. My husband and oldest daughter, Kate, joined me when they could. Despite the pain, I felt like I had something to bring to the situation because of my past experiences with loss. I could be somewhat of a teacher about suicide survival and how to deal with the crazy aftermath of such a shock. I was able to show Megan, Cory, and her family that while the grief is all encompassing, the intensity fades slowly over time and you miss feeling so close to the person you lost. In one way, it is a relief when you can no longer summon that intensity, but it's also fleeting because you aren't able to miss them as much year after year.

I met with my supervisor at Raytheon and told him that I would like to relocate to Huntsville. I believed we needed to be there to support these friends who had become just like family to us. The transfer was arranged, and we were reunited once again in the summer of 2019.

———

Through it all, from death to life, God has been so amazingly faithful, and you can rely on Him as I have to lead you on your journey. At the same time, I can confidently say that I have learned that you are ultimately in control of your own happiness. At the end of the day, if the life you are living is not bringing you joy, you can change that. What you do with your health, career, and relationships is up to you. I have brought in a lot of professionals, from life coaches to physical trainers, to help accelerate my growth as an individual. That's made a huge difference. I still feel like I need to manage my own destiny and make sure that my kids are provided for. That remains a carryover from my father's suicide and my mother's response to it, and I will likely never be able to turn those reins over to anybody else. I don't see it as a negative, though, and neither does my husband. Chris and I are living out the dream that I created in my youth to have a stay-at-home husband who would take care of the house and watch the kids while I went to work, and it's wonderful.

In addition, be careful to take pauses throughout your life, especially after a major event like a death, to ask yourself if you are where you want to be and where you want to go from there. On my fortieth birthday, in the wake of Elliott's death, I remember standing with Chris on the beach in Hawaii, and he asked, "If you could have anything you want and money was no object and you could dream any dream, what would you want?" Without hesitation, I said, "I would want another baby. I would want a bigger family." I was almost 42 when I gave birth to Kyle. Be open to new horizons no matter your circumstances or your age. Take a mindful pause to reinvent yourself. Move in the direction that fills your heart, and as you do, bring in a like-minded accountability partner to see you through.

To anyone who, for whatever reason, might be struggling with your direction in life, or even with despair or hopelessness to the point where you've considered ending it all, I say this: "I wish *you* could see you the way that *I* see you. I see you as a beautiful, successful person who has so much to give!" I know that is hard to realize that when you are sad or depressed, but as a survivor of suicide I can tell you that the person who takes their own life can't see the impact it will have on others. If they could, they wouldn't do it. It is a senseless act. People left behind in the wake of suicide feel completely helpless. My father took his life almost 30 years ago, and I still feel it every day. It's different as time goes on, but it is always there. Of course, my faith helps me. I sometimes sense my dad's presence in the same way I do God's presence. I feel connected to the people that are not here. My faith tells me there is a brighter day, the sun will rise again. I can always go back to the community of Christ, the people there that are like-minded, and know that they will always embrace me and love on me in a spiritual way.

How do you find and take control of your health and joy? One of the things I do is when I feel joy, I stop and say, "I feel joy." I literally say it out loud to reflect on those times and embrace and appreciate them because finding joy is sometimes hard to do amidst loss. In addition, bring in others to help you grow. Take pauses throughout life. There is no crisis big enough that it won't seem a little better after going for a walk. Be willing to reinvent yourself. Take risks. Be fearless. See what happens. Create a lot of crazy, fun life experiences.

As you do all these things and trust God in the process, you will become a leader who can overcome any challenge or obstacle that comes your way—and have a life worth living!

Amarie Whetten is devoted to inspiring women to find health and joy. She is looking forward to the next adventures God has in store for her and her family in Alabama. Contact Amarie at amariewhetten.jp@gmail.com.

8

Mindset of Joy

Melissa Morrison-Ellis

CHOOSE JOY, SING your song, and stay in the battle.

That's what I try to do every day to live beyond my challenges and tap into the real opportunity to unleash God's power and to make my present, and position my future, to be everything they can be.

It's a mindset I've developed along my professional and spiritual journey. I've attained some remarkable achievements as an engineer, such as being one of the first civil engineers and the first woman of color to graduate from the Gordon Institute at Tufts University M.S. in Engineering Management (MSEM) program in Medford, Massachusetts in 2003, and the first Raytheon employee to receive the Professional Achievement Award in Industry at the National

Women of Color STEM Conference in 2016. I believe God created me for a purpose, and I call upon His name whenever and wherever I need as the one who recharges and empowers me to overcome any obstacles that come my way. I've learned there is truth in the scripture of Philippians 4:13 that says, "I can do all this through him who gives me strength." It is with this strength that I approach my challengers, armed with a higher power, filled with His joy, and ready for any obstacles.

I've been told that my infectious chuckle and beaming smile are testaments to my purposeful choice of joy—and I'm grateful for that. Joy just doesn't happen. You can let every little thing around you leave you broken. Through your words, your thoughts, and your walk, you can be destroyed. Yet I get so much more out of each day when I start out happy and stay happy. I wake up in song. I can be overheard walking and humming a tune. It is that little piece that keeps me lifted up and ready for whatever lies ahead. When I have that song in my spirit and can keep it flowing, the smile comes with ease, and my joy is visible to others. That can also serve as sort of a defense mechanism. After all, it is difficult to attack a person who is smiling at you.

Joy is a natural part of me now, but it always wasn't that way. I was raised in an all-white area of Arlington, Massachusetts. I was the tallest, largest, and darkest in most rooms I entered. I was a bit shy, but I didn't realize how different I was from everyone else. In hindsight, I lacked presence. I enjoyed school. I did my homework, and I got good grades. I played the violin from the third grade through high school. I was a bit of a tomboy. I wasn't athletic, though I enjoyed gym class. I was always the bottom of the pyramid. Lined up with the boys, we'd get on our hands and knees to form the base, and they'd climbed up onto my shoulders and back. Then, on command, they fell down on me. In chicken fights I was always the carrier. Someone was always on my shoulders. Perhaps that was intended to help shape the strength I'd need to carry the burdens of my differences.

I was stronger from an early age, and that caused me to feel tough, even if I really wasn't a fighter at all. I was in fourth grade the first time someone called me a racial slur, and I knew it was an insult and not to be tolerated. I also knew enough to get my brother, Gary, who is three years older and had gone to the same school. That's what my mom had told me to do. That alone should've clued me in to how different I was. I was the only black kid in school until I was in eighth grade when Boston's metropolitan bus program dropped off students from the inner city. Before then, the only colored kids I knew were my cousins and one friend who was raised as a dark Italian.

I grew up pretty naïve. My parents, Pearl and Garfield, sheltered me, and at home I got plenty of love, direction, and guidance. Therefore, it wasn't until much later, when I was a young adult entering the workplace after college, that I became more aware of myself and how people reacted to me in the workplace and in the community. I recall the disappointment of not being offered the job interviews my peers of equal qualifications were offered and the shun of the salesperson in the Coach store who assumed I was just browsing when, in fact, I had enough money to satisfy his daily commission. It was during this phase of life that I had to figure out how to survive in the real world where acceptance was not freely given and began that shift to thinking, "No matter what life throws my way, I'm gonna be happy."

Choose joy.

Sing my song.

Stay in the battle.

———

My dad was a police officer in the city of Cambridge, Massachusetts. To earn overtime, he'd work details at particular sites for four to eight hours at a time, and he worked at quite a few construction projects. It was at one of these sites that he learned that engineering would be a great career choice for me because I was strong in math and science. I thought I was going to be a firefighter. That somehow made sense to me; my father was a police officer, so I'd be a firefighter. But my father pretty much told me that wasn't going to happen. He told me how grueling it would be to become a firefighter, and that engineering would certainly be a more rewarding choice monetarily. So, I agreed. I was in eleventh grade then and knew I'd be going to college for something. If it was going to be engineering, it was going to be engineering. My dad even told me where I should go to college. His cousin, the late David Blackman, was the dean of Northeastern University's Progress in Minority Engineering in Boston. I didn't challenge it. I knew my grades were good, and my cousin's friend was also going there for engineering, so why shouldn't I? That was how my career was launched, far different from the stories I later heard from high school classmates and coworkers who had received numerous sessions with their high school guidance counselor who assisted them in college selection, applications, and scholarships. I only saw my counselor when I skipped orchestra practice, landing me in detention.

Early on at Northeastern, I decided I didn't like the equations and repetitive nature of engineering, but I remained committed to it. After my second year there, I began its co-op program where I went to school for three months, worked for three months, then went back to school for six months and went to work for six months, extending my undergraduate period to five years. During this time, I discovered my love for the *management* of engineering versus the execution of engineering, and it afforded me the opportunity to study under a seasoned CEO and CFO in a large environmental engineering firm. Later, I transferred to the University of Massachusetts Lowell for a summer before finishing up back at Northeastern for two years of night school, earning my bachelor's degree in civil engineering. While in night school, I worked full-time at Anderson Nichols & Company in Boston, and gradually created a niche for myself doing things the technical teams didn't want to do but the business teams needed. I became the interface between the two entities, keeping the battle rhythm going. From there, I went to Scientists Engineers and Architects (SEA) in Cambridge, Massachusetts after being tipped off by a former coworker that they were good at engineering but could use some help on the performance measurement and execution side. They needed someone with a skill set created for that very purpose.

I took my self-developed toolbox filled with tricks of the trade for the business side of engineering and went to work while starting to pursue my master's degree in business. I learned of the engineering alternative to the MBA and went to Tufts Gordon Institute, with SEA paying my way and earned my master's degree in engineering management. I eventually developed a network within SEA's biggest clients. I was at city hall working with the capital planning team. I was at the department of public works working with the city engineer. I was with the finance department working invoices and the planning department deciding what projects they were going to do. It was great. I was shaping the future infrastructure of a major city in Massachusetts.

But there was a problem. I wasn't teaching anybody how to do what I was doing. Most of the managers were middle-aged white men, and they were basically dependent on me. The company was doing great, and they were getting all the information that they needed, but they were not getting it from the people they were paying to provide it. They were getting it all from me. So, while I was enjoying my role and showing great value to the company, I was actually handicapping people from being able to report on their own performance.

They didn't tell me any of that, though. I had to figure it out on my own. Sadly, before I did, I was told that an internal reorganization was going to eliminate my position. I was surprised—and angry. "Well, what are you going to do without me?" I asked my chief operating officer.

"You've got a bit of a chip on your shoulder," he replied.

Never at a loss for words, I quickly responded, "It's a boulder, not a chip."

The reality was my arrogance had led me to believe that they would fail, but that was so far from the truth—and I learned from that experience that being a valued leader is not about being the smartest person in the room, or the one with all the information, or even the go-to person. It's about taking your toolbox and training others on how to use the tools, and holding them and yourself accountable to ensure they have a chance to be successful and grow. Out of that, you will grow.

But for me to grow and then truly mature, I needed help, and I found that help through my faith. There I was, trying to figure out what I was going to do next. I was unemployed and had more free time. Already involved in my church, I was working in the food pantry there and helping to serve meals to the community twice each week. Anybody that wanted to come could get a hot meal. I found that serving the homeless, hungry, battered, and dependent—the truly downtrodden in the community—was so rewarding. I recall a woman coming in well after the meal was served. She had an infant in a stroller and another little one at its side. "Do you have anything I can give to my babies for dinner?" she asked. Though to do so outside of mealtime was against policy, I went to find something after first finding paper and crayons for the oldest and juice for the empty sippy cup of the youngest. I was quickly able to pull something together, and I sat with the family while they ate. The woman was so thankful. It had cost me nothing except for some time, some boiled noodles, and the leftovers I had set aside to have for my lunch the next day.

I also discovered that I really liked working with that group at the church and started going to weekly Bible study. Through that, I deepened my fellowship at Massachusetts Avenue Baptist Church in Cambridge, the same church I'd attended with my family since I was a toddler. One Sunday,

I felt the call of God to be saved. I didn't even stand up. I just sat in my seat as a warm almost numbing sensation came over me while the room itself seemingly fell silent. I completely tuned out of the world and tuned into the moment. Sensing what was happening in my spirit, I humbly responded, "Yes, God. I am ready." Shortly after that, I went into the pastor's office and declared I was ready to be baptized. It was just like that. When I committed myself to have a relationship with God, I began to recognize how I had been executing my plan for my life, but not making time for God to shape me into what He created me to do: to serve others humbly, selflessly, and to His glory, not mine.

That was when I consciously started choosing joy and finding my song.

From there, I ran my own business where all I did was go into organizations and create schedules for them. That lasted a short period of time, though, because I quickly realized I needed a little bit more structure to feel successful. I put a resume together, and I got picked up by a consulting firm that provided independent contractors for the Raytheon Company. I was brought on by them for a six-month program support contract, was later offered a full-time job, and I continue to work for Raytheon today. Those who have known me the longest can witness to my growing heart of joyful service. I no longer have to think about it. It flows from a desire God has placed within me to see happiness and satisfaction in others. He has given me direction, joy, and purpose, and I want others to have that same thing.

The boulder on my shoulder is gone. It has been replaced with a heart to serve, and from that service, I experience joy.

———

Throughout my career, I've been employed in male-dominated workplaces, and one of the challenges I've had to battle is the feeling that I have to constantly prove myself versus being taken at face value, or even on my past behavior and accomplishments. When I come to the table, I feel someone has already told the narrative of my story. There are preconceived notions. I wish people could instead see me more the way I see myself: fully equipped by God with everything I need to get the job done.

I am also in a place in my career where I work for a great company at a decent level of leadership. Are there days when I feel that advancing in my career simply isn't worth the battle? Sometimes. I definitely get tired of how long it takes to overcome the politics of sexism, racism, and other good old -isms where I feel I still need to prove myself to people and confront their preconceptions about me. But every time I think about stopping, I conclude that stopping is quitting, and if I quit, my challengers win. I can't help but think of the Norman Hutchins song, "Battlefield," that exhorts us to fight for the Lord, promising to serve Him until we die. That is my song! It helps me keep in mind that I need something greater to hold onto, that all of this is for a greater purpose, and if I can stay on the battlefield, I can achieve something larger. After all, the alternative to staying in the battle is overwhelming. The alternative doesn't get me out of bed. I want to keep my focus and apply big picture strategic thinking to everything I do. If I focus too much on the minute details and choose to major in the minors, I know I'm never going to be able to reach my goals and fulfill His plan for me.

The first step to developing that kind of strategic mindset, one that'll ensure you will never, ever stop but proceed to victory, is to develop your overall career journey roadmap so that you can focus on the joy down the road, the big win! Think of it as reverse planning beginning with the end in mind. You don't need to know exactly how you are going to get there, but you start with the title or role you see yourself achieving. Next, you research the open job listings to determine the required skills, years of service, attributes, licenses, and degrees needed. Then you work backwards, filling in the experiential learning and opportunities required to reach your goal. With your roadmap developed, you can return to it to see where you are and know, even though there is a challenge in your current battle, you are on the path to your goal. It's like that light at the end of the tunnel. It was through my skill set of planning for technical and municipality purposes that I became self-reflective on how to plan for myself, and it works.

Most importantly, I want women to realize that they were created for a unique and divine purpose—and God does have their back. I've shared with co-workers that I report to a boss much higher than my boss and their boss. It is a little snarky, but it is also a good reminder of who really is in control. I am not afraid to bring Him into my life in the workplace. It may be through song or even a moment of meditation in prayer. We are to know ourselves well enough to know when to ask for help, either from God or from other trusted leaders or co-workers. Don't be ashamed to do so whenever you are in need. People who don't know when to ask for help are never going to be truly free themselves as leaders.

One way that you can discover God's purpose for your life is to begin serving others, just as I did through my church's food pantry. It may be through mentoring in your nearby school or with the Girl Scouts or Boy Scouts, Boys and Girls Clubs, or at your church. You don't have to change everyone, but if you reach just *one*, that is more than enough to change a life. I spoke at a young girls STEM event. It took place during school vacation and was targeted to girls aged 8-12 to spark their interest in pursuing a career in science, technology, engineering, or math. I stressed opportunity, finances, fashion, fitness, and fun. I wasn't sure I had reached them until I later heard one of the young girls who attended my opening session on the evening news echoing some of the teaching I had shared that morning. *Got one!* I thought.

————

Three passages from the Bible are particularly inspiring to me. The first, James 1:2-3, reads, "Consider it pure joy, my brothers and sisters, whenever you face trials of many kinds, because you know that the testing of your faith produces perseverance." I learned this truth the time I was passed over for a promotion to a role I knew I was ready to do. I was very disappointed, but recalling this passage made me understand that maybe I wasn't as ready as I thought I was and that it simply wasn't the job for me. In time, it turned out getting that promotion wouldn't have been the career-rewarding event I thought it was. Others who took that role struggled, and if I had got the position, I would likely have faced the same difficulties.

The second verse is Romans 15:13. It declares, "May the God of hope fill you with all joy and peace as you trust in him, so that you may overflow with hope by the power of the Holy Spirit." Many people are told hope is not a strategy, but it most certainly is when you have faith. This verse was brought to life for me when I needed to hire a program manager. I put out the job requisition and had begun interviewing candidates when I got an email from a gentleman that said, "Hi Melissa. We met at the symposium last week. I noticed that you have a job opening. I'd like to apply."

I responded, "Sure, that would be great. Send me a resume." He did, and it was immediately clear that I would've hired him in a minute, but he was overqualified for the position. I decided to interview him and started by asking the obvious. "Why program manager? Why this program? Why now?"

I didn't anticipate his response. "I wasn't looking for a job," he revealed. "I had no plans on moving. I just started a new job—but when I saw this job under your name, I said 'I know her. She seems so happy doing what she does.' I want that."

Your joy will be attractive to others. It will attract and retain talent. It will attract other leaders to your side who can sharpen you and move you further along your roadmap. I was filled with all joy and that joy overflowed with hope to that man who wanted to work with me even thought he was overqualified and wasn't even looking for a different job. That is powerful.

Thirdly, Psalm 30:5 tells us that "weeping may stay for the night, but rejoicing comes in the morning." You can rely on joy. In fact, joy is a state of mind, a settled state of contentment, confident in hope. I have discovered that "joy" appears nearly 90 times in 22 books of the Old Testament, and almost 60 times in 18 books of the New Testament. That tells you joy is important to the Lord because He knows it is vital to your life.

So, choose joy. Sing your song. Stay in the battle. As you do, God will reveal His big picture strategy for your life—and it'll take you beyond any obstacles that come your way.

Melissa Morrison-Ellis is a program manager and mentor who also volunteers in various STEM initiatives, leveraging her company's Black Employee Network and outreach through the Boys & Girls Club of Northern Alabama. She was recognized as one of only 12 leaders in her company to receive the 2019 Program Leadership Award and delivers program management training to early career leaders with management interests. As a Beachbody® coach, Melissa encourages women to maintain a balanced diet accompanied by a manageable workout regimen. Contact Melissa at melissamorrisonellis@gmail.com.

9

Breaking Down the Walls

Dr. Yvette Rice

"**MAYBE YOU CAN** teach the women and the children. But you *cannot* preach from this pulpit."

When I heard those words from my pastor and husband, Sam, I couldn't help but wonder. *How did I get to this place? Another wall, another obstacle standing in the way of God's purpose for my life.*

Whether it was in ministry, industry, or even the cheerleading squad, I have been used by the Lord to break down walls as a female—and why not, considering the incredible legacy of other women whose examples have enabled and inspired me to do what I'm doing today: helping women Learn to Live in Victory and Excellence through my own company, LLVE, LLC.

For as long as I can remember, I've felt God's hand on my life pushing me forward even when fear spoke the word "no" loudly to my heart. I pressed in even when I did not precisely understand why God chose to use me and other women in my family to shatter barriers regarding women.

It began with my paternal grandmother, Clotile Harris, lovingly known as "Mama Clottie." She raised two sons as a single parent and had the privilege of seeing all four of her granddaughters graduate with engineering degrees from various Alabama universities in the early 1980's. She was like a culinary chef, cooking elaborate feasts and setting out all of the fancy china for family gatherings. I don't recall a whole lot about my grandfather because they divorced when my dad was just three years old. Back then, especially in the south, most women stayed with their mates and dealt with whatever they had to in order to protect the relationship, but my grandmother did not do that. Mama Clottie made the decision she felt was best for her and her two sons, moving in with my great-grandmother and taking care of her, my father, and his brother. She was strong, bold, and proud.

My maternal grandmother, meanwhile, was only allowed to finish the seventh grade because of racism in the south, yet she was one of the organizers of the first Girl Scout troop for African Americans in my hometown of Decatur, Alabama. Her name was Eunice Balentine, a spicy little woman just under five-foot-tall. We had a special name for her as well, "Mama Eunice." Mama Eunice was a cafeteria worker at a segregated high school. Even with their lack of formal education, Mama Eunice and her coworkers were highly intelligent and steadfast in their principles, imparting much wisdom to the young people they served each day. Mama Eunice and my grandfather, Leroy, were married nearly 56 years before my grandfather died, and they had nine children together. She believed that no matter what other people think or say, you cannot let that stop you from being who you are supposed to be—as I would find out from her in a very special way later on. Strong mentally and spiritually, Mama Eunice had a voice, and she was going to be heard.

Then there's Annie Ruth Harris, my mother. Her steely resolve to go from working as a teacher's aide to becoming an educator with a master's degree while working full-time, attending college, and taking care of our family during the early 1970's remains an inspiration to me. My father, Maurice, recognized her strength and respected it. He let her be who she was and still is. After serving in the military as a cook in Korea, he went to trade school and became a courier for a local bank. This was difficult for my mother because women during that time did not want to seem like they were domineering or moving faster than their husbands. Yet she accepted the call to be a teacher and wanted her children to see that no matter where you start, you can achieve whatever you desire.

My mother was a role model. She worked during the day, and when we came home from school, she helped us with our homework while still doing her own homework for college. After first attending junior college, she went to Athens State University at night to get her bachelor's degree in elementary education, then went and got a master's in education from Alabama A&M University. I believe my mother would have pursued a doctorate, but she felt our family had sacrificed enough for her to go to school. By then, my sister,

Gloria, and I were close to finishing high school and getting ready to go to college ourselves, and she wanted to be available to ready us for that transition and for our adult lives.

For her to accomplish what she did and to persevere was also exceptional because of the barriers of racism and sexism that she faced in a culture being transformed by the civil rights and women's liberation movements. Back then, there were still restaurants in Decatur that expected us to go to the back door to pick up our food. At the movie theater, The Princess, most of the African Americans sat in the balcony instead of on the first level. I remember one event that really opened my eyes about boldness. My mother's sister, Vernette, took me to the movies and refused to sit in the balcony. I don't recall anything about the movie, but the courage instilled within me after that incident is unforgettable.

My mother and grandmothers gave me quite a heritage. Each one was always there for me and encouraged me, and I took strength from watching them be strong regardless of the circumstances they encountered. In fact, their pioneering spirit of being among the first to do what they did was passed on to me and manifested in my life when I became the first African American cheerleader in the history of Austin High School in Decatur.

After desegregation began, I was given a choice. I could stay in my original school near home or go to a different one. I was bullied at my neighborhood school because my mother was always on the other children to try to get them to better themselves. "Your parents think you are better than me," they'd say. Tired of it, I decided I wanted to go to a desegregated school. I was still in elementary school then, and my parents and grandparents had taught us to love people regardless of race, family background, or whether they were rich or poor. So, I started a lot of friendships at my new elementary school that carried over into junior high and high school, and by the time I got to Austin High, many of the black children I went to school with at my neighborhood school were there, they knew me, and they had grown out of their bullying.

I decided to try out for cheerleader for the first time in middle school, and I didn't make it. That was discouraging, but I did not let it stop me. When I tried out again the following year, I made the squad. By the time I got to Austin High, they had black athletes on their sports teams, but they had never had a black cheerleader. Nevertheless, I tried out, the students voted on who made the squad, and I was elected because I not only got the votes of the black students, but also the white students who had become my friends. When we first started practicing in the summer, one of the other cheerleaders told me, "I've never been around a lot of black people before." I responded, "Well, I've never been around a lot of white people in this particular close situation before, so we'll get along fine."

We did, too. We went to each other's homes and had sleepovers. There were a couple of incidents that I had to deal with, but I was who I was and when I shared how I felt, we came to an understanding. Our relationships quickly grew beyond the barrier of our skin color—so much so that the next year, they chose me to be the captain of the squad. Another African American girl had joined us by the time I graduated.

Today, I'll still go to the football games at Austin, and

it is wonderful to see the almost equally-ethnic squad on the sidelines. When some of the girls find out I was the first African American cheerleader at the school, they want to talk with me and ask me what it was like to break down that barrier of racism, and I am more than happy to tell them all about it.

In the Bible, David faced a lion and a bear before he faced Goliath. This first wall was my lion, and it prepared me for the next two to come.

————

Because I was an Honor Society student and good grades came easily for me, I went off to the University of Alabama in Tuscaloosa thinking college was going to be a piece of cake. I received a minority scholarship to study engineering there because the school was trying to attract more women into the profession. But I did not look at the fact that I was a female going into an environment that was predominantly male, nor did I yet recognize the limitations I had as engineering student because of what I had not been allowed to study in high school. Back at Austin, the girls took home economics as an elective, and the boys took machine shop. That's just how it was. Therefore, when I got to college, the male engineering students had already been doing drawings and drafting, but I had never penciled a mechanical sketch. All of us girls were housed at Tutwiler, a dorm with an entire floor established just for the female engineering students to live on. The dorm provided tutors and study groups to make it easier for us to adjust to the engineering field, but it was difficult for me to learn to see things in a three-dimensional way because of my lack of experience with drafting. Plus, when I first began at Alabama, it was all about Coach Bear Bryant, Crimson Tide football, and having a good time. I hate to admit it, but my focus was not on school and academics.

That changed the day one of my engineering professors, a white man, looked me smack in the face and declared, "You may as well go and change your major because you will never be an engineer. You are not going to make it." I am sure what he said was more about my grades in the engineering department than anything else, yet his words made me feel as though he was looking down on me like I was nothing.

That was eye opening to me for a man, any man, to stand there and try to tell me what I was and was not going to do. At first, I went home and had a pity party. But then I remembered what my mother and grandmothers had always said that "a pity party is a party that no one wants to go to but you," and every bit of the strength and gumption they had modeled rose up in me. My mother and grandmothers also had the saying, "I can show you better than I can tell you."

I had never failed at anything in my life, and I was not about to start. I buckled down. I began hanging out with Robbie, a black football player who was majoring in civil engineering, which was no small feat in its own right. I hit the books instead of partying—and in two years my grades turned completely around. I was in the civil engineering department specializing in petroleum engineering, and I don't recall there being any black male students in the petroleum department. But some of the other white male students befriended me and helped me. They saw my capabilities, and they considered me to be a fellow student, not a black female. It was beyond my expectations. In the end, my grades were not stellar, but they were strong enough to get my degree. My mother kidded, "Everyone else graduated magna cum laude, but you graduated 'Thank you, Lawde." God had constantly been involved in my life from day one.

I had no plans to return to Decatur to live. However, the oil industry plummeted in 1982, so I had to move back home. Even the top students in my class were not getting job offers. Over the next year, the rejection letters came fast and furious in the mailbox, and at one point I thought I would never get a job. I heard people mumbling behind my back, "It must be her grades," or "She must not have taken enough math, so maybe she didn't really graduate after all." I tried to have another pity party, but my mother and grandmothers wouldn't have it. Even my father joined them in telling me, "You got that degree. Nobody gave it to you. You earned it. Regardless of what it looks like, you deserve it, and you are going to get a job."

Isaiah 40:31 directs us to wait on the Lord, but I did not want to wait. One day, my sister and I took her sons to the Birmingham Zoo. We ran into another black female engineer who had graduated with me. She said she had gone back to school, took some mechanical engineering courses, and got hired right away. That was all I needed to hear. I signed up for a mechanical engineering class at the University of Alabama in Huntsville, about 20 miles from Decatur. Just when I felt I couldn't wait any longer, one of my mechanical engineering classmates told me he was employed by the federal government at Redstone Arsenal, and that they were looking for female engineers. "If you want to fill out an application," he said, "I'll turn it in for you."

Within a few days I was called in for an interview. The woman who interviewed me said, "I'm sending you to this place first. If you don't like them, just come back here. I have another place for you to go. But before you leave here today, you will have a job." I went from no opportunity to picking the opportunity that I wanted.

That was miraculous to me, and I realized then that God had used the time that I was unemployed to mature me and make me realize it wasn't just Yvette.

He had a hand in my success and would for the rest of my life.

So, I got my first job at Redstone Arsenal in Huntsville as a mechanical engineer in the structural engineering group, developing missile systems and light composite prototypes for different organizations when fiber optics first came out. I was a young, excited engineer and was widely accepted—except by one older white male engineering technician who was not ready, not just for black female engineers, but *any* women engineers. When I did my first real design concept, I drew it up and turned it in to him.

He didn't even really look at it, but got out his pencil, marked it up, and stated, "We are not going to use this."

I knew it was really that *he* didn't want it to be used, but despite my disappointment, when I returned to my desk, I meticulously removed all his markings, cleaned it up, and put it in the drawer.

This won't be used, I thought, *but it's mine. It is my first work as a paid engineer.*

Less than a week later, the project office announced it wanted to use the design that matched up with my concept! The group did not know it had been marked up by the engineering technician. I pulled the drawing out of my storage desk and haughtily walked over to him. I'll never forget the look on his face when I slammed it down on his desk and walked out. That changed his opinion of me, in part because I never told anyone what he had done, but also because he saw that I was not going to be intimidated by him, or anyone else for that matter. I showed respect for him in front of the others, and we eventually collaborated on a couple of projects.

Overcoming that instance of gender-driven disrespect was the second wall I broke down, the bear that I overcame.

I carried on as an engineer for the next 10 years. During that time, I started dating my former Sunday school teacher. Sam was the man of my dreams, and while we were so very different, I knew in my heart he was going to be my husband, and I believe he realized it as well. After Sam and I married in Decatur, I decided to leave the workforce and began a new role in life—as a full-time mom—that would cover the next 15 years and set the stage for the biggest battle of my life as a woman.

My Goliath was coming, and the conflict was going to play itself out within the four walls of my own church.

———

I had our first child, Sharné, and she was two years of age when my husband accepted God's call into the ministry as a pastor. At the same time, God started tugging on my heart to also go into the ministry, but there was a problem. We were in a church denomination that did not approve of women being in ministry roles. I knew that, and to a certain level had accepted it, but it seemed like every time I picked up my Bible, two verses popped out. The first was Jeremiah 1:5, which reads, "Before I formed you in the womb I knew you, before you were born I set you apart; I appointed you as a prophet to the nations." The other was Ephesians 4:11-12. "So Christ himself gave the apostles, the prophets, the evangelists, the pastors and teachers to equip his people for works of service, so that the body of Christ may be built up."

I knew what God was saying to me through those verses, but I countered, "Lord, do you understand the churches I have grown up in all my life?" I did not want to violate church precepts, and I also wanted to submit to my husband as I felt the Bible taught. Yet the Lord would not stop, until one night I was in my living room praying and the peace of God just melted me. I heard Him so clearly. He said, "You didn't choose me. I chose you." I knew then that no matter what my husband said or the people in my denomination thought, I had to do what God was telling me to do. When I stand before the Lord on the Day of Judgment, none of the people who disagreed with me will be there with me. It will just be me and Him, and I wanted God to say, "Well done," not "Why didn't you do it?"

Then the Lord inspired me further, leading me to the story of Abigail in 1 Samuel 25. She had to completely bypass her husband in order to protect him and their entire household from David. She boldly did what God told her to do even though it meant going against everything she was allowed to do in that culture as a woman. From then on, I adopted the attitude, "Call me Abigail. I am doing this!"

From that moment on, I started getting invitations I didn't seek to speak at women's conferences. It did not matter that I was not ordained. I went and spoke, the fire of God hit me, and the power of God fell. I was so elated—until I came home. It was like the Ice Age there, so I never talked about what happened at the events. I just kept it to myself. Somehow, word always got back to my husband, and for the next several days all I got were one-word answers to everything. "Yeah." "Uh huh." Looking back, I know God was working on his heart, but I was miserable, and I told God I could not keep on living that way. I had a literal walk-in closet that I used as my prayer closet, and I went in there on my knees and cried out to the Lord.

"I can't do this!" I pled. "It is tearing my house apart. It is tearing up my family, and you do not call us to tear our family apart." But God was using me to pull my husband out of his comfort zone. I just did not realize it at the time. I remember praying in my despair, "I just want to die, Lord. Just let me die." And I was. The Lord was crucifying Yvette even while He was dealing with Sam. God showed me that I had to get out of the way. It did not matter what I thought. He wanted to use me as a pioneer to open the door to other women, so I needed to die and get out of the way.

After that, following the birth of our son, Samuel Christopher, my husband accepted a pastorate, meaning I was the pastor's wife in a denomination that doesn't believe in women preachers. One of my husband's nephews, a pastor, contacted me about a year later and said, "Yvette, God told me to invite you to come to my church and preach."

"Oh no, no, no, no," I replied emphatically. This wasn't for a women's conference. It was for his Sunday morning service. *If my husband is not speaking to me when I come back from a women's conference, I know he is not going to have much to say if I preach at a church during Sunday morning.* I refused the request, but he kept calling back. "The Lord won't let me get anybody else. It has to be you."

Desperate, I mentioned it to Mama Eunice, my maternal grandmother, the spicy little cafeteria worker. "You know what?" she said. "I am going with you." She never left her home church on a Sunday. She sat on the Mother Board there. She never missed a service. So, when she said she was going to go with me, I knew that I was supposed to do it. I went, I preached, and people gave their lives to Christ while others renewed their walk with God. It was amazing.

On the way home, Mama Eunice, who was in the same church denomination I was, was vehement. "Baby let me tell you. If God called you to preach, it doesn't matter what man says. You've got to obey Him."

From then on, if I was asked to preach or God told me to go somewhere to minister, I went and my husband dealt with it, usually with the same quiet coldness. Meanwhile, at the church itself, I took a back seat as much as I could and faithfully served him and the congregation, but I knew there was controversy among many of the members about what I was doing as that crazy Abigail preacher woman out doing her own thing.

A couple of years passed. Then my husband preached a message one Sunday morning out of the book of Matthew. The message was about how Jesus told Peter to get out of the boat. When he was finished, he announced to the congregation, "There is somebody here today, and God is calling you into the ministry. You are afraid to get out of the boat, but God's telling you to get out of the boat."

I held on to my pew. I was not getting up. I was not saying anything, and I was not going to go down there.

To this day, I don't remember how I got to the altar, but I went. My husband could have fainted. When he gave that invitation, he was surely expecting one of the guys to respond, a deacon or someone. Yet there I was.

When we got home, I asked him if he was shocked.

"Yeah, but when I saw you stand, I knew God said it was you." He then shared with me how he was feeling the burden of being a senior pastor, had been praying about it, and how God had told him He was going to send him some help.

My husband accepted me responding to the call to help him in ministry, but he was still wrestling with it because he knew it was going to change the dynamics of that church and his pastorate. A little while after that, God woke Him up in the middle of the night and took him from Genesis to Revelation, showing him every instance where He used a woman in the Bible. Of course, Abigail was among that parade of women in Scripture.

By the time I woke up the next morning, Sam was already up, so I just got up, got dressed, and we went to church. He told me he wanted me to sit on the front row, and I said I would. Before he began preaching, he told everyone in the church, "I need to do something." Then he looked right at me. "Yvette, would you stand up."

Adrenaline surged through me, and I hoped I wasn't going to collapse right there on the spot.

Guess what my husband did? He publicly apologized to me, and then revealed how God took him through His Word and showed him every time He had used a woman. "Who was I to tell God who He can or cannot use?" he said. "God can use anybody. I have been wrong all of these years."

Within a month, we had two other women ministers besides me in that congregation.

We stayed there for another year-and-a-half before starting New Genesis Community Church, which is where we created a leadership program for congregants and other ministers and continue to be used of God—as husband and wife, man and woman—today.

The third wall, gender bias within our church denomination, tumbled down, and it was because Sam and I slew Goliath together.

———

I was content just serving at the church, and I even wrote my first book, *Mountain Moving Made Easy*, but right after our son turned 15, I felt God telling me to get my professional resume ready. He had yet other plans for me. I knew I could not go back into the workforce as an engineer because of the amount of training I'd need to take to make up for the gap in time since I last worked. But I could return as a program manager because that's what I was doing when I left—and, sure enough, the Lord opened the doors for me to be a program manager for a government contractor for the United States Army Corps of Engineers. I ended up traveling nationally and overseas to teach others how to use the Corp's computer processing system. I had been out of the technology field for 15 years, but the Lord helped me and my team every step of the way.

I also found out that God sent me to the Corp to mature

me as a leader as I took John Maxwell training to better myself, and to be a light for Him in the marketplace. Some of the women working under me were Hindu, and I was careful never to talk about God or try to preach to anyone. Still, they knew I was a minister, and they came to me one at a time. One woman asked, "How do you pray? Every time we have a problem, I know you are praying, and it always gets fixed." That provided an opportunity to tell her about Christ, and I did. I told her how I prayed. She started coming to me more often, asking me to pray with her. It was incredible.

Within seven years after that experience with the Corp, I again felt God leading me, this time to start Learn to Live in Victory and Excellence, LLVE, LLC, which I did in 2015. When I returned to work, I observed so many people doing things because they had to, but they were not doing them with *joy*. I felt like I could make a difference by helping people to find their niche, the thing they love and would do no matter what. One of my first clients was a school superintendent, and before long I was coaching him and some of his school principals. After our sessions, he announced that he was retiring. He told everyone it was my fault because he realized that he had done all he could do as a school administrator, and that it was time for him to go do what he really wanted to do. I had helped him find his niche.

Today, I'm doing professional development training for technical leaders and for professional women. I now do more women-only leadership workshops for ladies who are business owners or company executives, and I use a forum where they can be open and unafraid to speak about what is troubling them or where they need to grow. That has created opportunities for me to coach female owners and executives one on one.

Again, it is amazing what God is doing in me and through me as I obey Him and lead when He tells me to lead. Are there more walls to be broken down? Only He knows that for sure—but I'll go in confidence with Matthew 5:13-14 as my inspiration. I love how it reads in the The Message version of the Bible. "You're here to be light, bringing out the God-colors in the world. God is not a secret to be kept. We're going public with this, as public as a city on a hill. If I make you light-bearers, you don't think I'm going to hide you under a bucket, do you? I'm putting you on a light stand. Now that I've put you there on a hilltop, on a light stand— shine! Keep open house; be generous with your lives. By opening up to others, you'll prompt people to open up with God, this generous Father in heaven."

God said for us to go and be a light in the marketplace. He didn't say take a big Bible with you and wear a big cross. He wants us to live the life before others. That's why He told me to call my company LLVE. The only way to Learn to Live in Victory and Excellence is to be in Him first. I don't tell people that. They figure it out after they are around me for a while.

————

As I speak with women, especially young people, about the challenges they'll face as they pursue being leaders in today's world, I tell them that the greatest obstacle for me has been getting men who are presidents of companies or larger corporations to see that I have value, and that the things I share equate to the same knowledge a man possesses. We've had men in high political offices who have said anything they want to about a woman, and it was perceived as nothing more than locker room talk. There is still a trend in our culture that says, "Just give women enough to satisfy them, and that'll keep them quiet." Yet we are in an hour when we are discovering we have a voice and God is going to make sure that we are heard—whether it is in the church, the marketplace, or the political arena.

In addition, changes are happening in the corporate world where women who have not been given proper opportunity are starting their own companies and succeeding. I know there are other leadership training companies similar to LLVE where the men who lead them are getting paid more than me simply because of their gender, but that's turning around. More and more, companies are saying, "We want Yvette. We want her to come and do training. Pay her what she is worth."

In his book, *Winning*, Jack Welch wrote, "Leaders inspire risk taking and learning by setting the example."[1] Dr. Myles Munroe defined leadership as being "the capacity to influence others through inspiration motivated by passion, generated by vision, produced by a conviction, and ignited by a purpose."[2] In retrospect, God used every life experience and challenge I faced to expand my abilities to passionately inspire others to take risk and knock down the walls that stand in the way of their pursuit of purpose.

If you know your purpose and what God has called you to, don't give in to the critics or anyone who tries to hold you back. Do not give in to fear. Stop listening to that voice of doubt saying it can't happen, and just trust God. Sometimes you just have to "do it afraid," but God will give you the voice to be the woman He wants you to be if you just keep moving forward.

All of the things I went through in life—and the strength that came from my mother and grandmothers—were preparing me for where I am right now. I want to pass that strength on to my daughter and granddaughter, Emery. I even tell my daughter-in-law, Amber, "You may have married into the family, but you still have that strength because you are connected to us." We are called to do whatever God has assigned us to do. It might not be easy, but we have to look at the legacy of the women who have come before us and made a way.

I know this, too. I am not leaving this earth until God says, "Okay, Yvette, you've knocked down enough walls. Come home."

Dr. Yvette Rice is owner of Learn to Live in Victory and Excellence (LLVE, LLC) and co-pastor at New Genesis Community Church in Decatur, Alabama. Yvette uses her visionary leadership ability, training expertise, and inspirational speaking gift acquired from over 30 years combined experience as an engineer, program leader and trainer for the Department of Defense, and government contractor for the United States Army Corps of Engineers to help others realize their true capabilities and maximize their potential. With her husband, Bishop Sam Rice, Th.D., their mission in ministry is to proclaim the Gospel of Jesus Christ to the unsaved, the outcast, the bruised, and the brokenhearted. Contact Yvette at yvette.rice@llve-llc.com.

Notes

1   Jack Welch, *Winning*, 2005. Jack Welch, LLC. HarperCollins Publishers. New York

2   Myles Munroe. Wisdom from Myles Munroe. 2012. https://www.facebook.com/MylesMunroeInspiration/posts/defining-leadershipleadership-is-the-capacity-to-influence-others-through-inspir/309419475805266/

10

....

Each One Reach One

Odetta Scott

IT'S BEEN IMMORTALIZED in song and adopted by organizations, and why not? It's a saying that truly says so much.

"Each one reach one."

For me, it is what drives me as a woman and as a leader to fulfill my God-given passion to better myself and others. As an author, advisor, mentor, and lecturer, I have been positioned to fuel the development of individuals through my activities with organizations such as Advancing Minorities Interest in Engineering, the Society of Women Engineers, and as a Science, Technology, Engineering, and Mathematics (STEM) ambassador. I've also done this through my 20-plus years of work experience in aerospace and defense, from mechanical design through program management, and in my current position as a senior leader at a Fortune 500 aerospace company, where I'm responsible for developing and implementing strategy for non-product supplier performance excellence.

And to think it all started back in my preadolescent years when I decided I wanted to be an astronaut. Something about the uniqueness of the career, the hard work it would take to attain it, and the reward it would bring excited me. I constructed a plan to meet my lofty goal, taking advanced math and science courses throughout my school years that not only satisfied academic requirements but served to set me apart from my classmates. I needed to excel. I knew my attitude, behavior, and work ethic would help set the stage for what I wanted to achieve.

In 1987, when I first heard Mae Jemison (the first female African American to go into space) had become one of the 15 candidates NASA selected out of more than 2,000 people to enter training to become an astronaut, I was elated. To know that a role model who shared my ethnicity, gender, and aspiration was on the path to accomplishing what I wanted so badly was encouraging. As I followed Mae's progress, I left my home in Vicksburg, Mississippi in eleventh grade to attend a magnet school in Columbus, Mississippi to enhance my education. That decision forced me to grow up fast without my parents or family, become more self-aware, and make new friends, contacts, and networks. From there, I attended the U.S. Naval Academy in Annapolis, Maryland (as most astronauts at that time were trained in the U.S. Navy) through my sophomore year before moving on to Texas A&M University to finish college and earn my degree in mechanical engineering technology in 1995.

My time at the Academy was bittersweet. The program provided much needed structure and discipline, and I successfully completed my plebe (freshman) year, which most consider to be the hardest. I am very proud of this accomplishment. However, towards the completion of the following year, I began to experience severe medical issues. I was in and out of the hospital, and doctors could not determine the root cause. I did some soul searching and determined that I was sacrificing my health to get a better education. My family was far away and not able to come and be with me as I was ailing physically with no clear diagnosis of what was wrong. During this time, I leaned in to God and grew in my faith. It taught me that when things don't turn out as we thought they would, there is still a greater plan in motion: God's plan!

By the third hospital stay, I realized I wasn't going into space like Mae did aboard the Space Shuttle Endeavor in 1992—but I figured I'd do the next best thing as an engineer by helping send others up and giving myself more visibility within the field in the process. I didn't complete my time at the Naval Academy, but resiliency and determination were added and reemphasized as building blocks for my life. It all served as a catalyst for my positive attitude and approach, and to make "each one reach one" a reality in and through my life. After leaving the Academy, I still had a few more medical episodes, but they eventually ended without ever being diagnosed.

As I entered into corporate America, this developed further and I realized I drew energy from applying analytical and problem-solving skills to different challenges. That helped me develop a successful career in operations, engineering, program management, and Six Sigma expertise for major aerospace and defense businesses. That energy also propelled me to find my true calling—positively adding value to the organizations I have worked for, and ultimately the people I have touched, by being an example and inspiring others to maximize their potential.

I decided, as Mahatma Gandhi said, to "be the change that you wish to see in the world."

To make "each one reach one" a reality in and through my life.

———

Christian faith had always been a part of my life as my mother and father ensured that me and my older sister and brother attended church and became knowledgeable of God and His love and salvation. My parents did whatever needed to be done to make sure that my siblings and I had whatever we needed. My mother worked two jobs for roughly 10 years, and I grew up in close proximity to cousins. We had love, food on the table, a roof over our heads, and each other, and that was enough. We did not realize we had less than others until we were much older. I was saved while I was in elementary school, went to church regularly, sang in the choir, and volunteered my time. But it wasn't until after I left Vicksburg to go to school in Columbus that my faith became real to me. I began to study the Bible quite a bit as my own journey and personal relationship with Christ started to take flight. I had to find a way be excellent in the classroom, keep my wits about me, and remain grounded. My spiritual journey provided that avenue. I was by no means an angel. I did not love Him then as I knew I should. I did not study the Word as I knew I needed to, and I engaged in some behaviors—gossiping, backbiting, lying (just to name a few)—that were not Godly at all. But as I began to learn more about God and know Him better, my behavior got in line with His desires for me. I rededicated my life to Jesus, renewed my commitment in thought and deed to be an example for Christ, and was baptized a second time.

Today, faith is one of the core values that inform who I am and how I live, along with integrity, authenticity, and character. I see character as the ability to stand strong in the midst of the storm and still do the right thing, even when the right thing may not be popular. Authenticity comes from having an awareness of who I am as an individual, and that self-awareness allows me to understand my own truths, trust in them, and learn from them despite the pressure I may be under. When you trust in yourself and in God, it is outwardly manifested as confidence because you know He has you covered when you may not have all the answers. As Romans 8:28 promises, all things work together for the good of those that love Him.

I also believe everything happens for a reason. In my current position as a senior leader at top Fortune 500 aerospace company, I recently met a group of highly motivated and talented African American women who are employed at the same company. They are much earlier in their careers, and the experiences that I have had as an African American woman in a male dominated field serves as both a connection point to these ladies as well as a role model. Whatever challenges they have or will encounter, I can tell them with certainty that they can achieve their goals because, as Scripture declares, we are "more than conquerors" through God.

When you are going through challenges or facing obstacles, you may not understand why and you may not accept it. You may feel hurt emotionally or physically—but in hindsight it was all orchestrated by God. Without those experiences, you wouldn't be the person you are today. You can learn from every situation, even if you consider it a failure. As Romans 8:28 assures you, "We know that in all things God works for the good of those who love him, who have been called according to his purpose." I try to live every day with that outlook, trusting in that promise. I once received some feedback from training I completed at work. Though I accepted it as a gift, it was not easy. It centered around my need to drill deeper instead of disengaging once I received the initial response about an issue that aligned with my recommendation or position. While I recognized the criticism, I did not fully understand the impact in both my personal and professional life. Being more aware now allows me to recall several instances where my behavior has changed, allowing that feedback to work for good.

As a leader, I've also discovered the importance of active listening with the intent of seeking to understand others. To be an effective leader, you have to meet your employees and your colleagues where they are and explain the "why" behind what you are doing in order to move your team and the organization forward. That is how you get that all-important "buy in" from people. You want to build loyalty so that they understand you are not going to lead them down the wrong path but will trust you. In the world of corporate mergers and acquisitions, change is inevitable. A company that is nimble, agile, and can manage change effectively has a competitive advantage because the only constant *is* change. In this environment, getting employees to understand the why is what will drive them in the right direction and assist in creating that agility.

Right now, I am part of a team developing a resource where women in technical fields can not only come, be comfortable, and talk about issues and challenges, but also trying to implement solutions to address those issues and the opportunities they present. As part of this process, I've needed to accumulate data and information, which includes sending out a survey to select women within the engineering technology realm, as well as a segment of men. As we navigate this process, we seek to learn information that'll help stimulate change at a deeper level. By doing this, I lead across my organization by influence. Changing a behavior based on positional power is not an option. In order to attain an increased response rates, we have to explain the why to the employees, help them connect the dots, and offer a value proposition that resonates with them. Then and only then will change occur.

I have encountered and overcome many challenges in my career. One of the most notable was when I served with a manager who had a totally different leadership style than mine. He was a more autocratic type of leader, very absolute and dogmatic, and he didn't resonate with me or my team at that time. I had about 10 people under my leadership who reported directly to me but also indirectly reported to the program manager. Being able to summon the courage to have a conversation with him about how his style was demotivating to the team and, therefore, would not net the results he wanted was empowering.

It took a while to break down the barrier for us to be able to work collaboratively, but over time, it became more of a reverse mentoring relationship where I provided insights to him. Sometimes he even pulled me in because he thought my leadership style would be more effective than his for a specific team or project. That experience has helped me in subsequent roles, dealing with other leaders, to be able to provide feedback in such a way that it is received as opposed to being rejected and things not changing at all.

Being a woman of color in what is still a male-dominated industry in engineering, I have found that I don't have to be liked, but I do want to have the respect for the value that I bring to my work and to the companies I have served. The skills that I learned to go in, make an impact, be respected, and still influence the process and drive it to the outcome needed have been very eye opening for me, and I am still learning as I go.

That makes it paramount for me to honor the concept of "each one reach one" in my position as a role model. I try to be an example by going out and providing exposure in the community. I introduce young women to the engineering field or recognize other women who are already doing something significant and making an impact. As ladies, we add incredible value. In all likelihood, it is going to be different from our male counterparts, but that doesn't minimize it. In fact, it should be elevated and fully appreciated for what it is. When you bring it to the table, you can integrate your different ideas into a solution, and that is what drives innovation. Research has shown that more diverse teams,

both in gender and ethnicity, are typically higher performing. Knowing what the Bible says about all the different
parts of the body working as one (1 Corinthians 12:12-26),
that's hardly a surprise.

———

My employer recently went through a merger where we
increased from about 24,000 engineers to 70,000—but
even after nearly tripling our number of engineers, there are
still very few women engineers. It is sad and awful, but as a
woman working for my company, supporting it, and recom-
mending it as a good company to work for, I am taking the
responsibility to work with other leaders in the engineering
field to develop the aforementioned program to help bring
qualified women into the employment pipeline and address
any other challenges we identify. What do we need to do in
order to keep and retain women? Why aren't we an employer
of choice for women?

Our leadership, led by our CEO, has signed up for
Paradigm for Parity, a global five-point action plan designed
to help companies accelerate the pace of achieving gender
parity. Based on extensive research and best practices, this
is the first set of specific actions that, when concurrently
implemented, will catalyze change and enable companies to
more effectively increase the number of women of all races,
cultures and backgrounds in leadership positions. Its ultimate goal is to make full gender parity (50/50) a reality by
the year 2030 within the executive ranks.

Through my involvement with the Society of Women
Engineers, I've discovered that women are graduating from

college with engineering degrees at a much lower rate than our male counterparts. One of the reasons that's happening is because girls are still unaware of or uninterested in engineering as an option for their lives. Working in under-privileged neighborhoods and schools via STEM programs, I've seen that kids may have dreams but not exposure to engineering and its prevalence. There is engineering every-where. We use our alarm clock to help us get up, but someone had to design that alarm clock—mechanical, electrical, the entire system. We just don't think about it that way.

In addition, girls typically don't grow up with an influence that steers them toward something like engineering or even the idea that it's okay to break something and learn to put it back together. Instead, traditional gender-specific issues or roles (Do you want to play with a doll? Do you want to get married? Do you want to play house?) are emphasized. When we do find young women who say, "I like math and science," they'll go on to say, "but I don't want to do that because I feel like I want to be a lawyer." They don't realize that involves more schooling than being an engineer, but they feel like becoming an engineer is too hard.

We've made some progress toward getting females interested and engaged in STEM (Science, Technology, Engineering, and Mathematics) careers. We are moving in the right direction. But not enough has been done. This makes me passionate to get more girls and young women directed toward engineering or similar career fields that remain dominated by men so that they can find oppor-tunities and be able to show the value they have and can bring to their workplaces. Previously, as a board member for Advancing Minorities' Interest in Engineering (AMIE),

I helped spearhead a program that engaged minority students in engineering and created a support system for both professional development and, in parallel, provided visibility to various corporations and scholarships for those students that became AMIE ambassadors.

There was one particular girl who joined when she was a junior in college and went through two cycles of being an AMIE ambassador. She was an African American female whose major was physics. When she went into her first corporate position as an intern, she struggled with being received for the value she could bring to the organization, as well as how she could get her colleagues to listen to her because she was the youngest in the group. I told her that when I experienced similar challenges early in my career, I came to realize that "you know what you know." Therefore, you have to go in with some level of confidence that your experiences are valid and that they do count. I also encouraged her to listen and ask questions and be willing to partner with tenured employees to learn from the knowledge they have acquired over the years. I told her they want to share and impart their knowledge, and that she couldn't go in wanting to change everything immediately with no understanding of the current state of the organization.

As a new or potential leader, remember that you can add value even being the newest member of the team. Be aware of who you are. Be professional in everything from how you engage with other employees and how you respond when someone gets under your skin. But I've also come to see that it's not as much about the direct value you bring, but about the greater impact you can have by *developing others*. You are only one person, but if you reach out and develop

20 other people, the impact and value can be maximized and optimized. To help others, you have to be able to ask questions that will cause them to identify "aha" moments and thoughts to uncover ideas and desires they may not be aware of yet. Seek to listen to and understand what the individual wants to do, and then ask questions to help them get there.

This process is not a one-and-done process. It takes time to develop. It is not for the faint of heart. Resiliency and perseverance are characteristics that have to be present for both parties. I suggest identifying someone that you can help or mentor within your community or workplace. Engage this person by being an active listener, getting to know them and truly understanding their desires. Share your experiences, both good and bad, to provide insight into different paths they could take, and help them develop an achievable plan to meet their goals. Hold them accountable and provide feedback along the way. When you do this for one person, the euphoria you experience becomes contagious. The investment of your time and energy is well worth the effort. I am currently mentoring several young female engineers at my company. One young lady recently shared that she really appreciated having someone there to assist her with challenges that she could not discuss with her supervisor, others in her management chain, or even members of her family. I listened, asked questions, and helped her determine the best next steps while becoming more self-aware and improving her confidence, knowing that she does and can add value. She expressed her gratitude to me, and I asked that she now pay it forward by helping the next person that came along in her path. Each individual that I help becomes part of my legacy.

———

There's a popular poem called "The Dash" by Linda Ellis. It's so beloved that it has its own website (thedashpoem. com) complete with products from wallet cards of the poem to jewelry, apparel, and free downloadable printables. According to the website, Linda wrote the poem "during a period when she was working for the top executives of a large and successful corporation with a strict and tense working environment. It seemed to her there were far too many worrying more about making a living than making a life." The poem's story of a man who spoke at a funeral and told of the significance of the "dash" between the dates marking the beginning and the end of a human life "have convinced mothers to spend more time with their children, fathers to spend more time at home, and people to reunite with long-lost loved ones."

I encourage you to find and read Linda's poem—for it had a tremendous impact on me regarding the legacy I want to leave in the "dash" of my life. I want to be the catalyst for something amazing in someone else's life. How many people have I really been able to influence?

That's what I ask myself each day as I continually strive to honor and to fulfill the idea of "each one reach one." I hope you will, too.

 Odetta Scott begins each day with a passion for living through her God-given purpose to better herself and others. An author, advisor, mentor, and lecturer, Odetta has fueled the development of individuals at all levels as well as driven transformational culture in professional and business settings. Contact Odetta at http://linkedin.com/in/odetta-scott-58298513.

11

....

Follow the Leader

Dr. Jana Lovelace

I LIKE BEING busy.

Or, at least I used to.

Today, I am more aware, living in the moment, soaking in the present, and focused on my true priorities—and it's all because I am now following the correct leader.

My journey began in Decatur, Alabama where I was raised as an only child by a single mom who owned a family floor covering business and was also landlord to a number of rental properties. Being raised as an only child meant my mom and I were very close, and we were blessed to be able to have a comfortable lifestyle. But being an only child also meant sharing in adult responsibilities. Even as a child, I played a major role in caring for my ailing grandmother who required around-the-clock care. We took late night and very early morning calls to tend to unruly renters, which meant getting out of bed at 2:00 a.m. and meeting police at the properties. I mowed lots of grass in my grandparents' yard as well as at the business and at home. I ran errands, cleaned at home and at the business, and answered phones at the floor covering store. Work was what we did, and we were good at it. It was just me and mom. All of the duties were split between the two of us, and I am thankful for that. I developed a great work ethic, which I learned from my mother and my grandparents, and when combined with a pretty healthy stubborn streak, I was a determined and persistent, probably (definitely) to a fault. I may not have always been the smartest person in the room, but I was probably going to be the one who worked the hardest.

That became a theme that continued throughout my life, and I am super thankful for those years and the lessons they brought. They helped shape me into the person that I am today.

But they came at a price—and that was a learned busyness. I didn't know how to rest. I didn't know how to be mindful or enjoy anything. I just knew how to *do*.

That, of course, was *not* living. It was merely surviving as I moved from one task to the next. So, while I highly achieved and met most of my goals, I didn't really start living until I almost died. Twice.

It wasn't until then that I discovered how to quiet my brain and my body so I could do something like go outside and play with my kids, enjoying them instead of doing yard work at the same time.

It wasn't until then that I could truly enjoy my husband and our amazing relationship with one another.

It wasn't until then that I learned to have faith and discovered how to surrender, be still, and let *God* lead me instead of trying to lead myself.

I've discovered He leads me so much better than I ever did.

———

As a licensed clinical psychologist, I have a private practice called ReGroup Psychological Services, LLC. I am also co-founder with Jeannie Lynch (also featured in this book) of No Limit's Women's Conferences, LLC, an organization that exists to bridge the gap between life's struggles for women and spirituality. I tell people that I have the coolest job in the world as I take a front row seat to watch others change their lives in amazing ways as they learn to truly overcome difficulties such as depression, anxiety, trauma, and both substance and behavioral addictions.

The majority of my career was spent in service to our nation's heroes, first as a military psychologist at the Veterans Administration (VA) and then for the Department of Defense (DOD) as a psychologist for the United States Army. My focus in graduate school at the Georgia School of Professional Psychology was health/medical psychology, and I did my internship and residency at the VA Medical Center in Memphis, Tennessee. I loved the culture of honor there, and I had a great experience during my two-and-a-half years at the hospital. I primarily worked palliative care at the VA, caring for terminally ill veterans and their families.

I also trained many of the resident physicians on how to tell people they are dying or that they have a terminal illness.

Then, in 2010, I returned to Alabama after I fell in love with and married John, who was also from my hometown of Decatur. I'd sworn I'd never move back home. I wanted to live in the big city and do great things. But John (and his amazing aqua-colored eyes) stole my heart. So, I went to work for the DOD at Redstone Arsenal, a United States Army post near Huntsville. Given it was an active duty base, I began serving younger soldiers, a change from my previous work at the VA. I no longer provided medical psychology services, but I delivered outpatient mental health services for soldiers with conditions such as Post-traumatic Stress Disorder (PTSD) and depression. Though I was no longer doing palliative or hospice care, I discovered I was still delivering bad news. These soldiers had their brothers die in their arms. They had fought as they and their units had witnessed the unfathomable. They often do not come home to their loved ones in the same condition as they left. How could they? Those experiences while deployed changed the chemicals and structures in their brains. While PTSD is not a terminal diagnosis, and I am convinced full recovery from PTSD is possible with a lot of work in therapy and help from Jesus, it is still difficult news to give because the soldier and his family will have to cope with it at some level for the rest of their lives. Addiction, depression, significant anxiety, marital issues, and lingering physical issues related to the trauma are their reality. Their battle wounds are mental, physical, spiritual, and emotional—and they are real. The simple pleasures we all take for granted, like going to a restaurant with our family, attending a birthday party, taking in a ball game, or getting a restful night's sleep are all changed for a soldier struggling with PTSD because of his or her heightened sensitivities to sounds, smells, and even people. It changes the way they see the world, others, and themselves. Not only does that alter the soldier's life, but it affects all of their relationships. It is a hard thing, something the average civilian will never truly understand—and it was absolutely one of my life's greatest honors to be able to serve them because they have sacrificed so much for all of us.

I was at Redstone Arsenal for seven years, and by 2017, John and I had built a family with his 21-year-old son, John William, and our two children, three-year-old, Liza Kate, and four-year old, Locke. I was humming along, going and doing as per usual. I was super determined and task driven, with busyness seemingly hard-wired into my brain. With a full-time job and three kids, it was useful that I was accustomed to busyness. But being used to something doesn't always mean it's healthy.

Then came the fateful day in early March when I was co-leading a group of women to participate in a Spartan Race, a five-mile course that featured 23 different obstacles like climbing a wall or filling a bucket full of rocks and carrying it across a creek. I loved fitness, and the obstacles were demanding physically and mentally. I was training for our second Spartan Race, out on a routine run, when it happened.

POP!

It was as if a bubble burst in my head. With it came the most horrible headache I'd ever experienced, and I have a high pain tolerance. I can't put into words that pain that occurred every time I moved. I was nauseous and vomiting. Yet when

I went to the ER, they couldn't find anything. I immediately thought it was an aneurism, but I was told instead that I had a pinched nerve in my neck. I knew that was not the correct diagnosis. It took another two weeks, during which time I went back to the ER and to my family physician as the pain and vomiting got significantly worse, before returning to the ER for a third time. I then underwent a spinal tap, and the doctors found blood in my spinal column. They rushed me upstairs to the Neuro Intensive Care Unit (Neuro-ICU) and said I was indeed having an aneurism.

I was only 35. As I was being rushed to Neuro-ICU, I should've been terrified, but I remember having a genuine peace that told me I was going to be okay. I remember praying for God to allow me to make it home to my husband and three babies, yet somehow knowing He had already granted that prayer. I spent the next four days in the Neuro-ICU before being transferred to a regular room, but they still couldn't find the aneurism, and I was sent home. It wasn't until a week later, when I was sent to a neurosurgeon at the Vanderbilt University Medical Center in Nashville, Tennessee, that I was properly diagnosed with a non-aneurysmal subarachnoid hemorrhage—a brain bleed in a vein, not an artery. It wasn't as lethal as an arterial aneurism, which was why I had survived as long as I had. But the pain was real, and so was my recovery.

I was working long hours at Redstone Arsenal. I had to be at work before my children were up in the morning. I did not get to wake them up or have breakfast with them. I did not get to say our morning prayer over their day. I did not get to fix Liza Kate's hair, which may not seem like much, but her daddy was not particularly skilled at doing a little girl's hair, which is understandable since he shaves his head. Nonetheless, despite their sometimes homeless look, I sure did love him for trying. But hair aside, I was missing too much, and I knew that wasn't what God wanted for me. But I was afraid to quit my steady federal job to open a private practice where, if I had a no show, I didn't get paid, not to mention forfeiting good benefits and retirement. Yet that brush with death shifted my entire perspective on life—and more importantly on how to truly live. In April, I began making plans for a private practice where I would have more flexibility to be the mom I wanted to be.

Three months later, I started having severe stomach pain one afternoon following work. I drove myself to the ER, and they proceeded to run a series of tests. They sent me home and called me back the next day, saying it was my appendix and that I needed to come in right away for surgery. Yet when I arrived, I was told, "No, we actually aren't sure. We want to send you for a colonoscopy tomorrow." Afterward, the doctor revealed, "I don't know what's causing your symptoms—but we just saved your life. You had a huge polyp that was precancerous. In less than three years, you would have died from colon cancer."

The doctor then assured me the symptoms that initially brought me to the ER were in no way caused by the polyp, yet those symptoms never returned. I am absolutely convinced the stomach pain was God's way to have the polyp discovered and removed. I haven't had stomach pain since—but through my pair of near-death experiences, I found out that I needed to follow a new leader: Him.

Sometimes God speaks to me in pictures. One day, I saw the image of a mountain and a pair of my boots (you know how much a good southern girl loves her boots) were at the bottom of the mountain. The boots reminded me of something I often said to my kids: "Put your boots on." They know that means, "Get ready. Let's go. We are going to work." Then God said, "Jana, you are not climbing this mountain by yourself, and you are not going to drag *me* up this mountain anymore. I'm trying to *take* you up the mountain. You have to follow me. You were never meant to climb this mountain by yourself."

That's what I had always done: trek up the mountain, get the problem solved, and get the thing done. But I had never prayed about what direction He wanted me to take. Prayer was my second reaction and hard work my first. As a result, I was pursuing things that, even if they were successful, weren't in His will or purposes for me.

In October, I turned in my notice and shortly thereafter left Redstone Arsenal to open ReGroup Psychological Services, LLC. I knew I had to be obedient to God, and I was banking on His promise to bless my obedience.

———

I have heard it said, "If the enemy can't make you sin, he will make you busy," and, boy, did Satan love to make me busy. When I was following my own mind, will, and emotions, I fell straight into his trap of "doing" and not "being." The result of that busyness was that it took my focus off of God as well as other priorities He had placed in my life. It made me lose sight of His blessings and those ever-present "God moments" because I was hyperfocused on my to-do list. That was not His intention for my life—and it is not His intention for your life, either.

Proverbs 1:31-32 talks about rebellious independence— and that's exactly what I had all of my life. Typically, when I trekked up that mountain by myself, it was not in a spirit of pride. It was not that I thought I knew better than God. It was merely a spirit of busyness and rushed pressure, the tyranny of the urgent, that caused me to not take the time to stop and pray. I charged up the mountain without consulting Him. I thought I didn't have time to wait for an answer. Most of the time, it wasn't even a conscious decision. I just did it. Work. That's what I did. Yet the Bible tells us to fully rely on God and not on our own wisdom or strength. He instructs us to "be still" and wait (Exodus 14:14; Psalm 46:10), recognizing that He is God and that will He direct our every step.

I have learned to follow God as my leader and to trust that He will always show me which direction is best, which mountains to take, and which ones to pass by. I don't need those boots anymore.

After opening my private practice, God indeed blessed my obedience as most of my previous clients followed me to the new practice, which allowed me to start my practice with a heavy caseload. That's not usually how it works. I treat patients with a variety of problems such as addiction, anxiety, depression, eating disorders, marriage and rela-tionship difficulties, insomnia, chronic pain, adjustment to illness, and everything in between. I am a nontraditional therapist. While I care a great deal about how my client's feel, I do not focus a lot on the feelings themselves. Rather, I concentrate more on their thoughts, because if we can change the way they are thinking, their feelings will follow. The Bible instructs us to take every thought captive and make it obedient to the truth (2 Corinthians 10:5). I do not sugar coat things either. I want to get to the problem, set therapeutic goals, and make changes in their lives. We get things done and usually have a little bit of fun along the way.

I still get things done in life, too—but not in the same way I once did. The pressure is gone. I have vowed to savor every drop of life. I no longer find value in what was my overscheduled, exceedingly professionally-driven, long-hours working, multi-tasking self. Instead, I want to be present, settled, and mindful of the life I almost lost. Do I get it right all of the time? Goodness, no! Old patterns are hard to break. But I get it right more times than not, and when I feel the pull to overschedule, it's almost like I have an internal alarm system that blares, "Danger! You are doing it again." That awareness, and the willingness to change my behavior, have been the keys to finding joy.

In addition to my private practice, I have found a calling to help other women, particularly moms, find the best version of themselves—to truly *live* rather than merely survive. This includes making sure they enjoy the "sweet spots" of being a wife and mother so they can have a full life, one of contentment, peace of mind, purpose, and fulfillment. If we think about all the things we have to get done on a nightly basis—from endless piles of laundry, unpacking backpacks and packing snack bags and lunches, or tending to all the boo-boos—it is easy to get overwhelmed and lost in all the tasks and miss the good stuff, the sweet spots, of sitting with our children, playing with them, and simply *being* with them.

One afternoon I was at the playground watching as my children lined up behind other, unfamiliar kids to play follow the leader. That always makes me a little anxious. I want my children to be safe and careful of who they follow, to fall in step behind wise leaders. But it made me think, *How often did I follow my own ideas and agendas? How many times did I follow myself up that mountain instead of following my true leader?* Then I wondered how often God, as He watched me on this playground called life, cringed, just like I do with my own children, because I followed the wrong leader. Following the leader is hard, but it is easier when my leader is God. I know His character, and He can be trusted. He makes wise decisions and has my best interests in mind. It takes relationship to follow God as our leader. If we are not talking with God in prayer or reading His Word and being spiritually fed, we may not be able to distinguish His voice from others.

Hearing and recognizing His voice is hard when I am consumed with busyness. My children have taught me this lesson as well. I'll never forget recently when our oldest son was working on our vast property in the early stages of building a new home. It was noisy, and he was yelling across the way to get the attention of his two younger siblings—but they couldn't hear him. Even though his voice was louder and more robust, it didn't matter. But when I yelled just once for them, they immediately heard me. They knew my voice better because it was more familiar. They'd listened to it more often. I'm their momma! Whose voice are you most familiar with? Is it God's voice, or is the noise of all the tasks demanding your attention and the sounds of chaos and discontent drowning Him out? Just as my kids knew my voice, spending time with the Lord allows you to know His—and knowing His voice is your sweet spot with Him.

———

In the end, life will have its busy seasons. Some are busier than others. There are times when the main objective in my home is to divide and conquer. My husband takes one kid to the grocery store, and I take the other as we work on a school project. One of us gives the dogs a bath while the other bathes the kids. My husband has a full-time job, I have a private practice, and we own and manage a property management company along with another business that conducts women's retreats, all while being active members of our church. Yet we have children involved in soccer, ballet, and gymnastics, I'm a home room mom in both of my youngest children's classes. But all of it is a season, one that will come and go. It is not a perpetual state of being. It won't last forever.

When we are too busy as women or as a family, we will not learn what God wants to teach us. I have discovered that busyness is not an environment conducive to learning. I do not learn well when I am stretched too thin, and neither do my husband or children. It is when we develop balance that we live a fulfilling life. Balance brings perspective on the type of activities and priorities we should have, and fosters intentionality to make sure the tasks we are doing have a purpose and are in alignment with God's will. Balance also creates opportunity for rest and those mindful, quiet times that bring true value to our lives.

Being caught up in busyness is not the life Jesus has for you. He meant for you to wake up excited to do your work, and to find a way to love what you do and to love fiercely. He meant for you to pursue the passions He gave you. God knows the desires of your heart because He placed them there. If He has blessed you with a spouse, He meant for you to have a passionate and beautiful marriage. If He has blessed you with children, He meant for you to enjoy each season of their lives, even the hard ones. You can be ready for a season to come to an end yet still find joy in it. He meant for you to live like you mean it! In fact, He died in order for you to live! Don't waste His sacrifice on busyness.

It turned out He desired to give me more than I could ever think, dream, or imagine (Ephesians 3:20). I was simply not trusting Him with it. It is amazing what I learned when the life I loved was almost lost twice. I wasn't following Him. I was following my own desires. Even though they were good things, they were not God things. He had better things for me. But I had to have a brain bleed and a near-diagnosis with cancer to learn that! My husband often jokes that God had to literally hit me upside the head to get my attention. He's not wrong.

I tend to become super busy when I am not following God. Listen to the Lord. Take the time to hear His voice. Examine your life. What are your fondest memories? Are they the crazy-busy, can't-think-straight, so-much-to-do moments? Or are they quiet, still times shared by the fire, watching a sunset, or just sitting in the grass with those you love? Life does not hand those moments to you. You have to create them—intentionally.

I've heard it said that we must become a good follower in order to be a good leader. I may have doubted that principle many times in my life, but my struggles have proven it to be true. I had to learn to follow the leader. My true leader.

I suppose, then, that I am still busy. Busy following His lead.

Dr. Jana Lovelace says she has "the coolest job in the world" as she takes a front-row seat to watch others change their lives in amazing ways as they navigate the really hard parts of life. She enjoys spending time with family, fitness boot camp, traveling, football, coffee, design, and glitter. Contact Jana at jana@drjanalovelace.com.

Made in the USA
Middletown, DE
28 September 2019